"Kate Solisti-Mattelon and Patrice Mattelon have created the ultimate easy-to-read, easy-to-understand handbook for companion animal caregivers. . . . This book stands out from the burgeoning crowd of critter cookbooks, animal stories, and behavior psychoanalytical tomes by taking a far leap beyond them and asking the animals themselves what they need from us. Their down-to-earth style and honest approach will benefit all who read—and heed—their words. It's simply all about love."

> — JEAN HOFVE, DVM, former president of
> the Rocky Mountain Holistic Veterinary
> Medical Association

"How wonderful to read a book that we know regular, everyday pet owners will finally 'get'! Having read almost every book available regarding natural and holistic petcare, we can honestly say this is one that can be read and understood quickly and easily. . . . Not only did we find the information clear, concise, and understandable by nonprofessionals but extremely accurate. Kate and Patrice's knowledge and expertise in the flower essences in unsurpassed."

> — RANDY and PHIL KLEIN, Whiskers Holistic
> Petcare

"A comprehensive and authoritative book. A must for all those with genuine interest in the welfare of animals. . . . Since your animals can't read this, you should—an excellent book."

> — JOHN SAXTON, president of the British
> Holistic Veterinary Medicine Association,
> and PAT SAXTON, Honourary Fellow of the
> Radionic Association

"*The Holistic Animal Handbook* is a gentle, heartwarming introduction to principles of healing with our animal companions. It contains enriching stories plus specific information and tools on physical, emotional, and spiritual dimensions of animal care, including how to telepathically communicate with animals."

> — PENELOPE SMITH, author of *Animal Talk* and
> *When Animals Speak*

"As a cat breeder, I thought I knew a lot about feeding and rearing my brood—until I read what Kate and Patrice say. . . . With its engaging simplicity of style and wealth of new information, *The Holistic Animal Handbook* has changed my views forever."

> — DIANE FINCH, breeder, Folderol Scottish
> Folds of Distinction

THE HOLISTIC ANIMAL
Handbook

ALSO BY KATE SOLISTI-MATTELON

Conversations with Dog

Conversations with Cat

Conversations with Horse

Kinship with the Animals

THE HOLISTIC ANIMAL
Handbook

A Guidebook to Nutrition,

Health, and Communication

REVISED EDITION

KATE SOLISTI-MATTELON & PATRICE MATTELON

COUNCIL OAK BOOKS
SAN FRANCISCO / TULSA

Council Oak Books, LLC
2105 E. 15th, Ste. B
Tulsa, OK 74104

© 2000, 2004 by Kate Solisti-Mattelon. Revised edition
Originally published in 2000 by Beyond Words Publishing, Inc.

Design: Carl Brune
Cover Design: Eleanor Reagh

Printed in Canada

LIBRARY OF CONGRESS CATALOGING-IN-PUBLICATION DATA
  Solisti-Mattelon, Kate.
    The holistic animal handbook : a guidebook to nutrition, health, and
    communication / Kate Solisti-Mattelon and Patrice Mattelon.—Rev. ed.
       p. cm.
    Includes bibliographical references.
    ISBN 1-57178-153-6
    1. Pets—Nutrition. 2. Pets—Health. 3. Pet—Diseases—Alternative
    treatment. 4. Human-animal communication. I. Mattelon, Patrice. II.
  Title.
    SF414.S66 2004
    636.089'3--dc22
                                         2004016901

Cover photo credits:
Dog © Ryan McVay/Photodisc/GETTY IMAGES
Horses © Photodisc/GETTY IMAGES
Dog and Cat © Photodisc/FOTOSEARCH
Kitten © GK Hart/Vikki Hart/GETTY IMAGES.

To all human beings who have been, are, or will be willing

to create a partnership with the animals in their lives toward

a shared goal of health, happiness, and wholeness.

Contents

ONE

GOOD FOOD
FOR BALANCED BODIES

TWO

BACH FLOWER REMEDIES
FOR BALANCED EMOTIONS

THREE

Natural Techniques
for Balanced Living

FOUR

Interspecies Communication
for Balanced Relationships

Foreword

I first met Kate several years ago. I had heard her name from a number of my clients. She had referred these clients to me, and after they had brought their critters to my holistic practice, I knew I wanted to meet her. The work she was doing with these animals had been described to me as "animal communication," or "animal medical intuitive." I was told that she could actually listen to the animals and understand what they were thinking, feeling, and saying. Furthermore, she could get a sense about the animal's disease process. But it wasn't until a client brought a sick dog to me, following a telephone reading Kate had performed for this animal, that I had an opportunity to observe her work firsthand. After communicating with the animal, Kate had determined that the problem was with his spleen; to be exact, he had a large spleen. Kate told the owner in no uncertain terms that she should take her beloved friend to see a veterinarian for a thorough examination. Now remember, this reading had been done remotely; Kate had never physically seen or touched this animal.

When the large, lumbering Rottweiler entered my office, he did seem a little off to me. He didn't have that spring in his step, and there was a dullness in both his coat and his eyes. He had been brought in to see me because he had suffered chronic diarrhea for nearly two years. I examined this 120-pound dog and found him to be rather sensitive on his abdomen. I was unable to feel any of the organs inside as I am usually able because the dog was holding his stomach muscles too tightly. I was worried about what might be going on in his belly; that much discomfort usually means something's wrong. The next day we had an ultrasound performed on his abdomen and, unfortunately, found a large mass on his spleen! I was impressed that Kate had somehow sensed what was ailing this guy. We were able to surgically remove the dog's spleen and found cancer, and it was early enough to make a difference.

The diarrhea this dog had suffered from for years was the way his body was loudly crying out that something rather serious was going on with his state of health. The dog's health was out of balance.

Eventually, I met both Kate and Patrice, imagining all the while that they would have an ethereal glow to them and be walking several inches off the ground—with or without wings, I wasn't sure. Was I ever surprised! Their appearance was quite normal, their special gifts notwithstanding. What impressed me most about my first meeting with this loving couple was that they immediately made me feel comfortable—it was just so easy to be with them.

Somehow, Kate and Patrice have managed to transfer that feeling of comfort to this book. As I have read and reread this marvelous guidebook, I have enjoyed feeling their comfortable style. And so, too, will you enjoy this feeling of comfort as you learn more about how to bestow the gift of health on your pet. And in the process, you too will find health.

The Holistic Animal Handbook can give you guidance on how to keep your own animal's health in balance. You are going to enjoy this book. Your pets are going to enjoy this book. If you love your animals, and if you want to see them live their lives in optimal health, this material will give you the tools you need to achieve that goal. As a holistic veterinarian in practice since 1982, I know that the best way for your animals to become healthy—and to stay healthy—is by changing their diet to well-balanced homemade food; reducing the stresses in their—and your own—lives; avoiding unnecessary drugs, surgeries, and vaccinations; and by giving them plenty of unconditional love. In order for a pet's guardian to be able to provide this sort of healthy environment, it takes a lot of work and preparation. This wonderful book, produced as a labor of love by Kate Solisti-Mattelon and Patrice Mattelon, will walk you, step by step, through that process of health-giving.

But most of all, just enjoy this book, and hug your four-legged friends!

ROBERT SILVER, DVM

Acknowledgments

Cooperation is the key to happiness and success.
— ANT

We would like to thank every person who has believed in us and supported us in following our hearts.

Our appreciation goes to veterinarians Rachel Blackmer, Dee Blanco, Christina Chambreau, Don Hamilton, Jean Hofve, Amy Norton, John Saxton, Rob Silver, Joann Stefanatos, Sheila Tuler, and Pam Wood.

To friends and colleagues Susan Belsky, Wendy Chase, Alison Davy, Shelley and Peggy Donnelly, Lavender Dower,

Diane Finch-Smith, Penny Hubbard, Phil and Randy Klein, Barbara Ludt, Pat Saxton, Penelope Smith, Linda Tellington-Jones, Karen Whitman, and Celeste Yarnall.

To our families.

To all the staff at Council Oak Books.

And finally, to the countless clients who have believed that their animals had something to say and who were willing to ask Kate and Patrice to interpret for them.

Our deep gratitude goes to all the animals who sent their people to us and who taught us all so much about unconditional love.

Introduction

The Holistic Animal Handbook is the result of 12 years' work as a professional animal communicator. Over the years, I have found that there is a need for people to have tools to both understand their animals and help them be as healthy as possible. Healthy companion animals are better equipped to achieve their missions with the humans that they love. Educated human companions are better able to comprehend what their animals are about. All of us benefit from better physical and emotional health and a greater understanding of sensitive communication.

Our Story

I have loved animals all my life. My connection to animals and plants existed from the time I first laid eyes on the outdoors. My earliest memories are of mental conversations with animals and plants. As soon as I could talk, I told my parents what these beings were telling me. My parents told me it was just my imagination. By the time that I was three, I felt confused and different. Fortunately, someone stepped in to help. My father gave me a gorgeous orange tabby kitten. His name was Dusty. The moment we met, my heart swelled with love and joy. Dusty spoke to me thought to thought, heart to heart. He told me that he had come to be with me, to share life's experiences, and to guide me in telepathic communication with the natural world. He also told me it would be best to not share these things with my parents, as they were not ready to accept them. This made me sad, but it was a relief at the same time.

The next three years were full of wonder and miraculous encounters. We listened to the roses telling us about their love affair with the sun. We talked with turtles and learned how they can predict the weather. When I was five, Dusty urged me to dive into human relationships as I had done with nature. I did so reluctantly, because human duality made me uncomfortable. I preferred the honesty and purity of animals! However, by first grade I began to enjoy school and make friends.

One night as I was falling asleep, Dusty came to me and said, "I am proud of you. You have done so well. I love you very much. Our work together is done." I fell asleep with the sound of his purr, feeling that everything was well with my world.

The next day, Dusty was gone, run over by a car on a busy street nearby. I was devastated. I did not want to live without him. I blamed myself for his death. I got very sick with tonsillitis. In the hospital for a tonsillectomy, I was falling under the anesthetic. Just before everything went dark, I felt myself lifted off the table and cradled close. I smelled Dusty's familiar smell and noticed I was being held against soft, orange fur. I heard, "I am here as I always have been. Everything will be all right. It is not your time. You have much to do. I love you." Then everything went dark.

I awoke to a sore throat and a sunny room. I felt different. I accepted Dusty's message, but I could not bring myself to talk with the animals and plants. Without him by my side, it was too painful. By age eight my ability to "hear" had completely shut down. At last I was a normal kid—sort of. I never could forget the conversations I had with Dusty. As hard as I tried to forget, they stuck with me.

I grew up in northern New Jersey, attended private schools, and went to Smith College and the University of Michigan. Later, in my twenties, I saw a therapist to deal with my rocky adolescence and the usual baggage. In therapy, I discovered a part of me had been put aside. As I got in touch with this part, I began to feel things differently, to sense my intuition growing. Eventually, I began hearing the trees. Although it was unsettling, in that I had no external reference for talking trees, it felt perfectly right to my soul. I promised myself that I would continue to explore and develop my intuition. My journey took me to Santa Fe, where I studied alternative healing therapies and connected to gifted psychics. Soon, to my great joy, I was telepathically hearing animals again. I dedicated myself to continue to refine my abilities and to be of service to animals, their humans, and our planet. In 1995, I met Patrice.

Patrice grew up in France, the only son of hardworking parents. Because finances were tight, at two months of age, Patrice was put in a foster home. At age four, his parents reclaimed him. This experience shaped him to be self-sufficient and ultra-sensitive to his environment. He learned to pick up subtleties in unspoken communication. At age eleven, he started studying the art of fencing. He was exceptionally talented. Fencing further refined his abilities to sense the thoughts and moves of others. After a stint in the army and the achievement of his Master Fencer status, he taught physical education. During this period, he also began studying alternative healing therapies. The world of energetic medicine opened up to him. He discovered that he had a gift for hands-on healing. In 1993, he began to clairvoyantly receive information about the interrelationships among numerology, the tarot, and the Kabbalah. He developed this information into a sophisticated yet simple tool for personal and spiritual growth, which he shares with people eager to change their lives and create happiness and balance.

When we met in 1995, Patrice had had little exposure to animals. As we began to work together, he discovered how the animals responded to his gentle, healing touch. When in consultation with people and their animals, Patrice tunes in to the human beings while I act as an interpreter for the animals. Together, we help human beings see how their animals mirror them. We also teach people how to holistically care for and feed their animals. We put them in touch with holistic veterinarians and other practitioners, and provide suggestions, resources, and tools for personal growth. We feel very blessed to be using our talents and abilities to help people and their animals come into balance and into awareness of how they help one another.

This handbook is a compilation of information we routinely share with clients in private sessions, in lectures, and in seminars.

How to Use This Book

Our goal in this handbook is to provide simplified information and practical tools that can be applied and developed. The book is meant to serve as a starting point. If you practice and use the information, you and your animal will feel better and develop an even deeper interspecies understanding. At the end of the book, we include a resource section for those people interested in going into deeper detail. We are familiar with all the books, periodicals, shops, foods, and individuals listed in the resources and recommend them highly.

The Holistic Animal Handbook is designed to help human companions understand that physical, emotional, and spiritual balance and healing are important to companion animals. In each chapter, we address the animal's needs and issues as well as offer ways for each committed human to accommodate them. In Part One, "Good Food for Balanced Bodies," we provide valuable information not normally available from allopathic veterinarians and animal-care manuals. In addition to nutritional information, we present simple recipes and suggestions for supplements and ways each of us can immediately improve our animal's health and well-being. The first step in any healing program is correct nourishment. In Part Two, "Bach Flower Remedies for Balanced Emotions," we introduce readers to this extraordinary tool that can help animals stay calm, happy, and focused; heal quickly; adjust to changes; and more. The second step to health is balanced emotional well-being. Part Three, "Natural Techniques for Balanced Living," looks at relating to our animals in an entirely new way, or perhaps in the ancient way—as their mothers do when they teach them. Understanding how animals perceive and respond to their world and to us helps us avoid many misunderstandings, resulting in "behavior problems." Part Four, "Interspecies

Communication for Balanced Relationships," introduces the reader to telepathic communication, a tool for connecting mind-to-mind and heart-to-heart with an animal. In this chapter, we also support people in accepting the deaths of companion animals by explaining how animals perceive death and how we can learn from our animal's passing. Animals are connected to Spirit/Source/God/Creator all the time. Because they are not separate as most of us are, animals can teach us how to attain spiritual awareness and can help us heal our souls with unconditional love.

The Holistic Animal Handbook combines practical and esoteric information in an accessible format. We firmly believe that holistic healing—combining tools for physical, emotional, and spiritual well-being—is the answer for our animals and ourselves. As you learn to use these tools for the animals in your lives, we hope you will think about yourselves. If this book helps you on the path to holistic health, then we are supporting your animals in helping you! The circle is complete.

We hope that you will find this information enlightening. Everything in this handbook has been reviewed and approved by the many four-legged clients we have worked with over the years. They have taught us what they need,

and have helped us learn how to teach people to understand. So, for the dogs, cats, and horses in your life, and for
your own enrichment, may you use and enjoy this handbook to the fullest extent possible.

Good Food
for Balanced Bodies

CHAPTER 1

The Need for a Natural Diet

Eating is about engaging in life. Without good food,

it is impossible to be fully present.

— SAINT BERNARD

A balanced body begins with balanced nutrition. This simple fact was stated over and over to us in various forms from dogs and cats we would work with every day. When we'd be called in to consult on behavior or health problems, animals would tell us, "we feel tired, unable to focus, grouchy, intolerant, and hungry because we're not getting the food we need." Processed pet food was simply not nourishing them. What could be done to change this situation? Patrice and I began to do some research into what cats and dogs needed for optimum nutrition. We also began exploring what was actually in pet foods, why they were not complete and balanced nutrition as the labels claimed, and what health challenges developed as the results of eating processed foods.

We discovered that cats and dogs are in serious danger today from the processed foods we are feeding them. Many diseases—cancer, kidney disease, hip dysplasia, inflammatory bowel disease, FIP (feline infectious peritonitis), and FIV (feline immunodeficiency virus, or feline AIDS), to name a few—are devastating our pet population. Why are our animals developing diseases and allergies at such young ages? Cancer is now the number one diagnosed disease in companion animals.[1] Holistic veterinarians agree that poor nutrition is one of the leading causes of these problems. Many diseases are in large part a direct result of how we feed and what we feed our companion animals.

We believe that once caregivers realize what actually goes into pet foods, they will take action. If we are committed to having healthy animals in our lives, it is critical that we take responsibility for feeding them correctly.

Dogs and cats are descended from wild predators, which means that they are hunters. The prey they hunt for is other animals, which means that they are carnivores or meat eaters. Domestic dogs are descended primarily from wolves. Our dogs—like wolves, foxes, and coyotes—are classified as carnivores and carrion feeders. All of these canines are designed to catch their prey, rip it open with their teeth, and eat it raw. When these predators eat a variety of prey—deer, antelope, rabbit, grouse, mouse, and so on—they eat the organs, muscles, and sometimes the gastrointestinal contents. They eat connective tissue and bone marrow, finally crushing up small bones and cartilage. They eat as much as they can hold and then bury or hide the leftovers, including the bigger bones, for later. All canine species are part of Nature's clean-up crew, eating carrion or old dead animals and bones as well as fresh, live ones.

Domestic cats are classified as obligate carnivores, which means that they *must* eat meat. Our cats are descended from the African wildcat, *Felis silvestris lybica*, a savannah-dwelling feline who has limited access to rivers and seasonal exposure to intermittent streams and ponds. This cat absorbs all its required moisture from its prey. As savannah-dwelling carnivores, these felines subsist almost exclusively on rodents, birds, reptiles, eggs, and insects. This prey is also exactly what our cats are built to eat.

All predators have periods of "feast and famine," meaning that they catch something, eat it, and then often go a long time without catching anything. On the average, small prey meals are fully utilized within four to five hours. The predators' bodies are designed to be empty for a time between meals. This "famine" period allows their bodies to metabolize all the nutrients from their last meal and to empty their elimination systems so that unfriendly bacteria and parasites have no breeding ground. Nature keeps predators hungry to ensure that they will continue hunting. However, it can be argued that the body of a carnivore is healthiest when it's virtually empty. In fact, when cats or dogs do not feel well, they often fast to clear and clean their systems.

To feed our domestic dogs and cats correctly, it makes sense to feed them as closely as possible to the way nature designed them to be fed. So what exactly does this mean?

WHAT CATS AND DOGS NEED

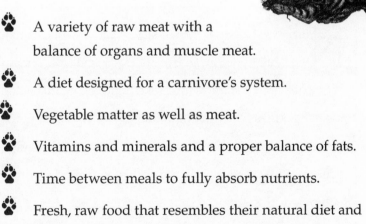

- A variety of raw meat with a balance of organs and muscle meat.
- A diet designed for a carnivore's system.
- Vegetable matter as well as meat.
- Vitamins and minerals and a proper balance of fats.
- Time between meals to fully absorb nutrients.
- Fresh, raw food that resembles their natural diet and contains enzymes critical for the digestion process.

HOW MOST CATS AND DOGS ARE FED

🐾 Dry food: Does this bear any resemblance to their natural diet? It is not fresh. It has very little moisture. It is cereal, not meat, based.

🐾 Canned food: Is there anything fresh here?

🐾 Food available twenty-four hours a day, as well as . . .

🐾 . . . treats between meals. This frustrates the carnivore's need to rest its digestive system.

🐾 Leftovers from human meals: We are doing better here, but everything is usually cooked.

Have you ever seen a wolf or a bobcat barbecue a rabbit, open a can of hash, or buy a box of cereal? Of course not. They are not designed to eat this way.

Nutritionist Celeste Yarnall states that raw food remains in the system for four to five hours; cooked food remains for eight to ten hours; and dry food takes fourteen to fifteen hours to make the transit from mouth to litter box. Remember that a carnivore's system will be overworked and prone to breaking down if congested by food, so any cat or dog on cooked or processed foods has a stressed system.

When we feed cats a diet of dry food only and allow them to eat whenever they wish, we are going against the natural rhythm of their systems. As obligate carnivores, cats must eat meat and animal fat. Dry food is grain based, which means that it is more carbohydrate than protein. Carbohydrates turn into sugar in the cat's system. The balance is upside down for a predator designed to eat meat. Also, cats' bodies are designed to absorb moisture from their prey. Dry food has little moisture, and cats are not built to drink water as dogs are. Without moisture in their food, cats are forced to drink, adding stress to the kidneys. Eating whenever they wish, or grazing like an herbivore, keeps their systems constantly working, leaving indigestible food in the digestive tract and supplying a fertile ground for bacteria and parasites. Extra pressure is put on the pancreas, digestive system, liver, and kidneys. One holistic vet informed us that she guarantees kidney trouble for any cat on a long-term diet of dry food alone. Typically, this diet wears out the body before its time and can lead to immune-system breakdown, organ failure, and other diseases.

CLEAN TEETH AND HEALTHY GUMS

Dry food and crunchy biscuits do not clean a carnivore's

teeth as the manufacturers would like us to believe. A cat's teeth are long and sharp, designed to puncture and tear. Cats have no grinding teeth, only a couple of molars in the back of their mouths designed to quickly crush the vertebrae of a prey animal. A wild feline's teeth are cleaned by their own highly acidic saliva while the cat tears and pulls at the prey animal it has killed, as well as by crunching bones and fibrous tissues of the prey's body. The cat's long, sharp teeth have no flat surface area for grinding, so when a cat bites down on hard, dry food, sharp pieces break off and lacerate the gums. Then the dry food leaves a sugary residue in the mouth. This is not only painful but contributes to tooth decay and gum disease.

Although dogs have a few molars capable of chewing, wild canine teeth and gums are kept healthy by scraping bones on the side of the teeth in addition to tearing, pulling at, and crunching their prey, as the felines do. As Dr. Jean Hofve comments, dry food is as effective a teeth cleaner for a carnivore as substituting toast for a toothbrush and dental floss would be for us!

To keep our dogs' and cats' teeth and gums healthy, we must (1) feed a raw-meat diet, and (2) give raw chicken or turkey necks or backs and/or beef-marrow bones (always organic or antibiotic-free, free-range) at least four times a week. Mollie, our Sheltie mix, inherited bad teeth and gums with which she suffered for six years. Within a few months of being on a raw-food diet and eating raw chicken and turkey necks, backs, and gizzards, and scraping those beef bones, her teeth were cleaner, her gums healthier, and her breath 100 percent sweeter!

Raw chicken and turkey necks and beef bones are easily digested by a normal dog or cat digestive tract. By normal, we mean a digestive tract with the correct stomach acids, digestive enzymes, and good overall health. However, if your animal has been eating processed foods only, has had antibiotics recently, or is ill or out of balance, raw chicken necks and backs and beef bones can cause stomach upset or worse problems. You can't expect a person used to subsisting on french fries and soda to be able to easily digest a steak and a salad! The digestive system must first be reconditioned and slowly accustomed to eating raw, nutritious foods. At that point, raw beef bones and raw chicken or turkey necks, backs, and gizzards will be a fabulous tool for dental health! For more on the benefits of raw chicken, see Dr. Ian Billinghurst's book, *Give Your Dog a Bone.*

Be very wary of rawhide chews. Not only do they provide negligible nutrition and fill up the stomach and intestines, but many of them are prepared under unsanitary conditions and carry parasite eggs. They may also be preserved with cyanide![2] Other commercial dog bones are bleached with chlorine.

WHY IS PROCESSED FOOD KILLING OUR ANIMALS?

If we listen to the advertisements for pet food, we hear repeatedly that such-and-such a food provides completely balanced nutrition for our cats and dogs. Because the manufacturers tell us this is so, we believe them. They also make it convenient and "economical" for us to feed our animals. Just open a can or pour a little dry food in the bowl, and it's done.

Besides realizing that processed food bears little or no resemblance to the natural diet of a carnivore, it's important to know exactly what is in the can or the bag. Here are some common ingredients to look for in the foods you are feeding:

BY-PRODUCTS: The Association of American Feed Control Officials (AAFCO) defines by-products as "the non-rendered clean parts, other than meat, derived from slaughtered mammals."[3] Pet food is the repository of the livestock industry's waste—parts rejected for human consumption. Sometimes this can mean parts of the animal such as liver, heart, kidney, tripe, and so on. However, the quality of these ingredients varies greatly. According to Dr. Hofve and others, whatever the quality of by-products, they are not meat and are not an adequate source of animal protein for our dogs and cats.

MEAL: The AAFCO defines meat meal as "the rendered product from mammal tissue exclusive of blood, hair, hoof, horn trimmings, manure, stomach, and rumen contents except in such amounts as may occur unavoidably in good processing practices." This often includes the so-called "four Ds": animals that are diseased, disabled, dying, or dead—before they reach the slaughterhouse. Even though the AAFCO definition precludes the presence of blood, hair, hoof, and so on, there is evidence that "meat meal" may include roadkill, pigs, and rabbits, as well as hair, feces and urine, dried ruminant waste, unborn calf carcasses, and more. Cancerous tissue; poultry heads and feet; spoiled, rancid, and moldy meat—all can be used in meal and passed on as "pet food." Meat meal is a composite product that has been ground and pulverized to remove most of the water. Poultry by-product meal is defined as "the ground, rendered, clean parts of slaughtered poultry, such as necks, feet, undeveloped eggs, and intestines, exclusive of feathers, except in such amounts as might occur unavoidably in good processing practices."

In 1989, an eleven-month-old child died from an allergic reaction to penicillin. The source of the penicillin was the dry cat food she regularly nibbled on. The levels of penicillin in the cat food were at least six hundred times the limit allowed in human food. Although pet-food ingredients are cooked under high heat to destroy dangerous organisms— not always successfully—they do not necessarily alter or destroy drugs like penicillin, pentobarbital, and others.[4]

CORN: Cereals are also not nutritionally adequate because they do not satisfy some essential amino acid requirements. Due to its high sugar content, corn is a major contributor to obesity and pancreatic problems like diabetes. Dogs and cats are not designed to consume vegetable or cereal products as the most significant parts of their diets.[5]

> Grains used in some pet foods are those rejected for human use due to poor quality, mold contamination, or pesticide residue.

SOYBEANS: Soy has been linked to gas in dogs due to the presence of starches, which dogs lack the enzymes to digest. Thus, it is not a viable form of protein.

PRESERVATIVES: BHA and BHT are petroleum derivatives that accumulate in the body tissue and may cause liver enlargement, increased risk of cancer,[6] and epilepsy in dogs.[7] These preservatives have been approved for use in human foods and cosmetics for preventing hydrogenated vegetable oils from going rancid.

ETHOXYQUIN: This preservative, manufactured by Monsanto, is a fungicide and color preservative. It was originally developed as a rubber stabilizer and a pesticide. Why is it in dry foods? Because it extends the shelf life of a product to twelve months or more. (Is this a good thing?) The so-called "natural" preservatives like vitamins E and C provide only seven to nine months of freshness. Thanks primarily to consumer pressure, Iams and Science Diet are removing Ethoxyquin from their over-the-counter foods, but as of this writing they are still adding it to their prescription diets. In addition, Ethoxyquin may still be present in some ingredients without being labeled. For example, fish meal, which is present in nearly all cat foods, may still contain large amounts of it.[8]

ALUMINUM: Almost all dry and canned foods go through aluminum extruding equipment, so these foods may expose cats and dogs to aluminum toxicity. The only way to securely protect your animals from heavy-metal poisoning in this form is to prepare the homemade diets. You will know every ingredient, since all will be prepared in your kitchen.

OK, now that you know what kinds of ingredients turn up in most pet foods, what can you do about it?

- Become a label reader.

- Learn what the listed ingredients are. See the resources for further reading.

- Take responsibility for feeding your pets better. See the resources for recommended foods and suppliers.

- Share what you learn with your friends, veterinarians, and the stores where you shop for pet food, and save more animals' lives.

CHAPTER 2

Solutions

Getting what you want demands

commitment and persistence.

— PERSIAN CAT

The best solution to the pet-food problem is to educate yourself on how to prepare the healthiest meals for your canine and feline friends. It is critically important to create a balanced diet when making food from scratch. An imbalanced homemade diet can cause severe deficiencies. Do not embark on making food for your animals until you have the proper supplements to balance the diet. Remember, the best homemade diet is a "duplication" of the nutrients available in a prey animal. In other words, the recipes below attempt to "build a bird," with its complement of essential enzymes, vitamins, minerals, fats, proteins, and carbohydrates. This is an excellent place to start.

Size, age, breed, activity levels—all of these factors and more figure in when developing a balanced diet. Not all vets and nutritionists agree on exactly what a balanced diet is for a cat or dog. In fact, there are tremendous disagreements between them. Instead of following too closely any diet designed by humans, we prefer to emulate nature. As mentioned previously, cats and dogs are predators and are designed to eat live prey. We believe that the best diet is created for individual dogs and cats as their needs indicate. Many years' worth of evidence supports the fact that a homemade mixture of organic raw meat, cooked fish, eggs, fresh vegetables, grains, enzymes, and vitamin and mineral supplements will provide balanced nutrition superior to any processed food. However, specific breeds of dog require specific types of meats, grains, and vegetables, as well as specific supplements. Certain meats, grains, and vegetables are not recommended for particular breeds. A breed-specific recipe chart is provided in the next chapter. You can use the recipes as a starting point, and get the advice of a veterinarian or nutritionist specifically trained in dog and cat nutrition to develop the optimum diet for your own animals. See the resources for holistic veterinarians' associations, books, and other sources on nutrition and preparing meals for our animals.

If you are not quite ready to prepare food from scratch, buy frozen prepared meals for your animals. All you have to do is defrost them and serve. Nature's Variety, FarMore, and Bravo are three excellent sources of frozen meals in a wide variety of meats, including ostrich, venison, buffalo, turkey, beef, New Zealand lamb, and rabbit. These meats are all human quality, hormone and antibiotic free. The mixtures contain ground bone and organ meats with some extras like fruits, eggs, and oils.

If you can't buy "homemade" frozen meals, at least find and buy prepared pet foods with the highest quality ingredients possible. Insist that prepared foods, canned or bagged, contain human-grade meats or, better yet, humanely raised, natural, free-range meat. Always add enzymes and vitamin and mineral supplements prepared for animals to help the animals absorb and assimilate as much nutritional value as possible. Please note that pet-food manufacturers may change a food for the better or for the worse with no notice to the consumer. Even if your animals do well on a prepared food, do not take for granted that it will remain the same over the coming months or years. Continue to read labels carefully for any changes. See the resource section for a listing of recommended brands.

Always check with a holistic vet or one specifically trained in nutrition before changing your pet's diet. Ask what their training consisted of when evaluating whether or not a vet knows anything about nutrition. Any vet can claim to be trained, as they all receive a little course on nutrition in vet school. For example, at Colorado State University, one of the largest veterinary programs in the United States, "Veterinary Nutrition and Metabolism," taught in the spring semester of the first year, is the only course on nutrition offered in the entire four-year program. This course consists of sixteen lectures. Veterinary students receive one one-hour lecture called "Introduction to Nutrition for Dogs and Cats," one one-hour lecture called "Evaluation of Pet Foods," and one one-hour lecture called "How to Read and Interpret Labels" (on pet-food packages). That's all they get on cat and dog nutrition. In many veterinary programs, Hills, the makers of Science Diet, offers the only nutrition "training." They certify veterinary technicians, who learn how to prescribe their "prescription diets." As a result, staff at a vet clinic may know a great deal about prescription diets, a little about what is in pet foods, but very little about what cats and dogs require nutritionally for balanced health!

When changing from one prepared food to another, always go slowly. Before changing anything, read up in one or more of the recommended books on what to expect and how to support the animal in changing to a healthier diet. Once you have read about what your animal may experience and how to support them through a change, you're ready to start. Here's a tried-and-true method of introducing new foods: Working with the normal portions of food your animal is used to, in week one, give one-quarter new food to three-quarters old. In week two, give half new food mixed with half old. In week three, give one-quarter old food to three-quarters new. In general, the same volume of fresh, homemade food will have half the calories of dry food. Substitute two cups fresh food for one cup dry. Observe your animal and how he/she is eliminating. Some changes may occur. If symptoms such as diarrhea and unusual shedding appear, introduce the new food more slowly. Cooked white rice by itself can be given as a stabilizing agent for the bowels. You can also make a mixture of one-half part ground beef or turkey cooked with the fat removed mixed with one-half part cooked rice with a dollop of plain low-fat yogurt. This provides simple nourishment and stabilizes the bowels. Always make sure that plenty of fresh water is available, and closely observe your animal to be sure that he does not dehydrate. If your animal is in any type of distress, contact a holistic vet immediately.

When choosing poultry versus beef and lamb or other meats, remember that most cats will do better with poultry, although "red" meat is good from time to time or when an elderly, anemic, or ill animal needs more energy. However, beef and lamb are deficient in the essential amino acid taurine, which stimulates the immune system and T-cell production. Taurine is necessary for dogs, critical for cats; hence, it is important that beef or lamb be fed alternately with poultry. Dogs will do well on poultry, venison, buffalo, beef, or lamb, but poultry, especially turkey, can be helpful for dogs that may be too energetic or aggressive. Don't forget to research where your dog's breed originated to choose the best-suited proteins, grains, and vegetables for them. Remember that in the wild, canines and felines eat a variety of prey, so varying meats, grains, and vegetables can be a good thing if your animal is strong and healthy. An animal with a compromised system cannot adjust easily to variety. Go slowly with any change until your animal's system is strengthened and accustomed to variety. Adding enzymes greatly enhances an animal's ability to adjust to and assimilate new foods.

NOTE: See chart on page 44 through 46 to choose the best meats, vegetables, and grains for your breed of dog.

ENZYMES: ESSENTIAL INGREDIENTS FOR GOOD HEALTH

Enzymes are special proteins that participate at a cellular level in every chemical reaction in the body. Digestive enzymes are present in raw foods, but they are destroyed when food is cooked. When we feed ourselves and our animals a diet of entirely cooked, canned or dry, processed foods, we have to rely on the pancreas to supply the missing enzymes. This extra stress on the pancreas leads to a great number of acute and chronic health problems.

What exactly do enzymes do? Enzymes are essential for maintaining proper functions of all parts of the body. Without enzymes, the body simply cannot support life. Digestive enzymes are *mandatory* for proper digestion and absorption of nutrients. Enzymes break down food particles for storage in the liver or muscles. Later, this stored energy is converted by other specialized enzymes to construct new muscle-tissue, skin, glandular, bone, and nerve cells. If digestive enzymes are missing from foods or present in inadequate amounts, the pancreas and other digestive organs must compensate. Symptoms of enzyme deficiency include diarrhea, constipation, gastritis, colitis, obesity, poor weight gain, arthritis, liver and bladder problems, excessive shedding, and oily or dry coats. Enzyme supplementation will benefit cancer, cardiovascular disease, hip dysplasia, and many other degenerative diseases. In other words, if an animal cannot absorb and utilize its food, many kinds of problems can result. Problems and imbalances occur typically in the digestive tract but also wherever there is a weakness in the body. Improper absorption of nutrients can make a cat or dog cranky, aggressive, lethargic, or unhappy and may also lead to inappropriate elimination and behavior problems. How would you feel if you were walking around malnourished all of the time? Most of our cats and dogs are malnourished due to the poor quality of the foods they eat as well as a lack of enzyme support to absorb and utilize their foods.

Enzymes aid in the elimination of toxins by the colon, kidneys, liver, lungs, and skin. They decompose poisonous hydrogen peroxide and free healthful oxygen from the hydrogen molecules. Enzymes help coagulate and concentrate iron in the blood. Like a thriving, busy ant community, enzymes are the working force that keeps bodies alive and functioning.

Most holistic vets and nutritional experts agree that any animal fed dry or canned foods at any time in their life needs to have digestive enzymes added to their meals. When preparing an all-raw diet, it is also important to add enzymes to help the animal's digestive tract adjust to and continue to absorb the new foods. A pinch, thoroughly mixed in just before serving, is all you need to start. If the cat or dog doesn't like the smell or taste at first, cut down to the tiniest amount and work up to one-eighth or one-quarter teaspoon per meal. (It's best to follow the instructions on the specific formula.)

So what do you look for in a good enzyme supplement? In our experience, the best digestive enzyme supplements contain the basic enzymes—lipase, protease, amylase, and cellulase—and may also include probiotics (friendly digestive bacteria) such as *lactobacillus acidophilus* and *bifido-bacterium*. These friendly bacteria keep the digestive tract healthy. They are particularly important if the cat or dog is undergoing antibiotic therapy or has been on antibiotics at any time. Most antibiotics destroy these friendly bacteria along with the unfriendly ones involved in infection. Essential fatty acids (EFAs) are also helpful to prevent hairballs and to help coats and skin stay shiny and beautiful. Celestial Cats Feline Enzyme Supplement contains taurine, a vital amino acid for cats. Taurine is available only in raw meats, and most cats and many dogs fed processed foods are deficient in it.

Fortunately, there are some excellent enzyme supplements available for companion animals. They include Celestial Cats Feline Enzyme Supplement and Celestial Dogs Canine Enzyme Supplement; FloraZyme EFA, FloraZyme LP, and FerretZymes Plus, developed by Dr. Russell Swift at Pet's Friend; PetGuard Digestive Enzymes; Dr. Goodpet Feline Formula Digestive Enzymes and Dr. Goodpet Canine Formula Digestive Enzymes; and ProZyme Digestive Enzymes. Whatever you are feeding your furry family members, always add enzymes!

We switched our cat, Azul, to a homemade diet including supplements specially formulated for raw foods, and in two days he was different! His litter box stopped smelling. There was 50 percent less waste in the litter box, because his body was using almost everything he ate. His coat became silky smooth. Best of all, he became more affectionate and outgoing. He began to snuggle and play more. It's logical to think that each of us is happiest when we eat, digest, and absorb what our bodies are designed to eat!

We were so impressed with the changes in both our cat and dog that we now teach "cooking" classes to show people how to prepare these simple recipes. We also produced two videos, *Save Your Dog! Nourish Him the Way He's Built to Eat,* and *Save Your Cat! Nourish Her the Way She's Built to Eat.* With the videos you bring our class into your home and learn how easy it is to prepare a balanced, homemade diet for your own animals. See resources for order information.

Another cat, Charlotte, a gorgeous orange Persian, was cranky and often difficult. Grooming her was so awful for both cat and human that her person felt forced to sedate Charlotte a few times a year in order to brush her! Having tried many ways and suggestions to help Charlotte be happier and calmer, her person finally made the commitment to change to a homemade diet. At first, Charlotte would not eat. It took months of persistent, patient efforts, mixing in "bribe foods," working with different ingredients, but eventually Charlotte accepted the new food. In the process, her personality began to change. She became friendlier and less reclusive. After a few months on the new diet, Charlotte's fur began to change. It became silkier, softer, and less prone to knots and hairballs. She even began to allow her person to gently brush her. These changes seemed miraculous to her person, but again, the correct diet will nourish and support all of us in very clear and obvious ways!

Because many processed dog and cat foods contain toxic ingredients and are killing animals daily, making food for our animals is not just "pampering" them. Homemade meals are saving lives! So, for the optimum health of your dogs and cats, the following chapter contains basic recipes that can be adjusted for your individual animals, thanks to Robert Silver, DVM; Jean Hofve, DVM; and Celeste Yarnall, Ph.D. Remember to check with a holistic vet before making any changes to your pet's diet. Expect some adjustments as you would with any dietary change. For further information on how and why these diets were created, see the resources for books on holistic health and nutrition. Eventually, your animals will be enjoying vibrant health!

WHY ORGANIC MEATS, GRAINS, AND VEGETABLES?

Organ meats must be from animals "naturally raised" on organic feed with no antibiotics or hormones. The liver and kidneys store and process toxins. If you feed your animals organ meats from cows and chickens fed antibiotics, hormones, and pesticide-ridden feed, they can receive major concentrations of these toxins. These concentrations of toxins can kill cats and dogs if they eat enough of these organ meats. (Read labels of processed foods carefully to control how much liver they are receiving. Liver is a major ingredient in canned cat foods.)

Cows and chickens raised according to organic standards have a much better life than their feedlot counterparts. Normally, they are fed pesticide-free, feces-free, sawdust-free feed, are given no antibiotics or hormones, and live in cleaner, less crowded conditions. Many of these animals are free-ranging or cage-free. Most are slaughtered via humane methods. As a result, their eggs and meat are cleaner and energetically much better food—for all of us.

Organic vegetables and grains are free of pesticides and chemical fertilizers. They, too, have energy that is more nourishing to our bodies. They have a life-force energy you simply do not find in factory-farmed vegetables.

Finally, buying organic foods supports farmers who are doing their best to honor the earth. Consuming foods that are grown or raised using sustainable, humane farming practices ensures that food will be available for future generations of humans and animals. We believe that this is the only responsible choice for those of us who love animals, our children, and the earth.

This information and these suggestions are offered to help you change your pet's diet for the better. Some people are concerned about the cost in time and money necessary to create a better diet for their pets. At one of our lectures, a woman with two large dogs voiced her fears about the cost of buying fresh organic food. Sitting next to her was a Lhasa Apso breeder, who said that when she switched from feeding fourteen dogs a quality dry food to the homemade recipe, not only did she have less excrement to clean up and less grooming to do on each dog, but her dogs got along better, and she saved money on food! The time and money invested in a proper diet will save lots of money otherwise spent on unnecessary vet bills and expensive medications and therapies. More importantly, it will provide a foundation in health and balance that will help your companion animal live a long, happy, and normal life.

You might be interested to know that in England, before processed food became available, Labrador Retrievers commonly lived to be twenty-two years old. Their diets consisted of prey animals, meats from the butcher, and their humans' meal leftovers. We recently met an Englishwoman whose family cat lived to be a healthy, happy twenty-two, as well. He died peacefully in his sleep one night. His diet? Raw kidneys and whatever he caught in the garden.

Lastly, we point out Dr. Francis Pottenger's ten-year study of cats. He studied some nine hundred cats on various combination diets. From the start, one group was fed raw meat, raw unpasteurized milk, and cod-liver oil. In contrast, another group was fed cooked meat and pasteurized milk. He observed the results of these two diets throughout several generations of cats. The cats fed raw food remained healthy, lived long lives, and bore normal kittens generation after generation. The cats fed cooked food developed behavior disturbances, various diseases, and poor-quality coats, and they bore malformed, unhealthy kittens that were sterile after one or two generations.[9] Please note that this was merely cooked food—not even processed food, which has even less bioavailability than cooked food! This massive study, largely ignored by the veterinary medical establishment, provides compelling evidence for preparing or adding whole, raw foods to our pets' diets.

Thanks to Dr. Silver, for his recipes and suggestions, and to Dr. Yarnall for her expertise in nutrition. Special thanks to Dr. Jean Hofve, for sharing with us her research on commercial pet foods and the nutritional requirements of cats and dogs. Thanks to both Dr. Silver and Dr. Hofve for their efforts to educate veterinarians, veterinary students, and their clients about the importance of proper nutrition for companion animals.

CHAPTER 3

Recipes

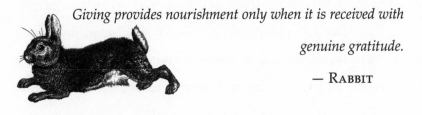

Giving provides nourishment only when it is received with

genuine gratitude.

— RABBIT

Below are two recipes that are easy to prepare and very simple to make in big batches to freeze.

FRESH-FOOD RECIPE FOR CATS

1 pound	Raw ground turkey, chicken, lamb, buffalo, beef, ostrich, or eggs (choose one)
2 ounces	Puréed raw vegetables or baby-food vegetables
2 tablespoons	Cooked grain
6–8 ounces	Purified water or broth, as needed
2 tablespoons	Oil
1 tablespoon	Food-grade bone beal with red marrow, or Dr. Silver's Calcium Balancing Powder (see recipe on page 47), or a vitamin and mineral supplement with calcium, designed for cats

Pinch   Feline enzyme supplement, sprinkled over food
            and mixed in just before serving.

For cats, the basic ingredients are 70–80 percent meat
(protein + fat) and 20–30 percent veggies and grains. Visualize a mouse.

Mix all ingredients until you get the consistency of a
thick chili. Add more purified water or chicken broth as
needed.

Once the basic recipe has been accepted, introduce a
small amount of organic organ meats daily (one part organ
to five parts muscle), or serve at least three times a week.
Mix chicken and turkey with poultry-organ meats, beef
with beef-organ meats, lamb with lamb-organ meats, and
so on. Liver, kidneys, and heart must be from animals naturally raised on pesticide- and antibiotic-free feed since liver
and kidneys are detoxing organs, and you don't want to
pass toxins on to your cat. Cut organ meats into bite-sized
chunks with sharp knife or scissors.

You may include bribe foods to entice your cat to eat,
such as sardines; anchovies; organic baby-food chicken or
turkey; canned mackerel, tuna, or salmon; or cooked chicken
or turkey. It's okay in the beginning to cook the meat a little.
Gradually cook it less and less until it's just lightly seared
and/or serve cooked meat mixed with raw if possible, and

then add supplements and oils. Another option for chunks of meat is a quick dip in rapidly boiling water.

For vegetables, use raw zucchini, carrots, yellow squash, broccoli, green beans, peas, parsley—or cooked winter squash, yams, pumpkin, or other vegetables of your choice. Do not mix several different types of vegetables for cats. Use only one or two of these at a time. Leafy greens should be steamed and pureed due to competitive binding with calcium and iron. Garlic is great in small amounts, especially during the spring and summer to ward off biting insects. Don't use onions.

For grains, use oatmeal, barley flakes, rice, millet, quinoa, spelt, or rye, cooked to a gruel-like consistency. Cooking grains in broth gives a better flavor. Use one grain at a time. Grains may be eliminated entirely. Add more veggies; or substitute one four-ounce jar of organic baby-food vegetables or four ounces of baked sweet potatoes mashed in a little butter for vegetables and grains.

For oil, use cod-liver, salmon, flaxseed, hempseed, or walnut oil, or a combination of one fish and one other. Fish oils are best for cats.

It's ideal to model ancestral eating habits, so leave food down no longer than forty-five minutes, morning and night.

Offer food three to four times per day for two- to four-month-old kittens and pregnant or lactating cats.

Food can be kept in the refrigerator for two to three days. Store in covered glass or plastic containers, or zip-lock bags. It's okay to prepare large quantities and freeze in serving portions. A great way to make mouse-size portions is to spread the recipe in an ice-cube tray, freeze then defrost one or more cubes as needed. Also, zip-lock bags can hold one or more day's meals and be frozen in quantity.

Do not freeze more than twice, and try to refreeze within a few hours of mixing up the food. You may add supplements before freezing, but it's better to add them after defrosting. Enzymes must be added only at serving time. It's also better to add the delicate oils just before serving, as they can be compromised by freezing. It's always better to defrost in the refrigerator rather than leaving food to defrost on a counter, and never microwave anything! Microwave ovens disrupt and change cell activity in the food and possibly in the digestive tract as well. They transform the protein molecule shapes, altering nutritive value.

Most importantly, prepare and serve with love.

How much should you serve? It stands to reason that the ideal serving for a cat is the size of an average mouse—

approximately two tablespoons. We feed our cat one mouse-sized portion each morning and night. Some cats will require larger portions, especially in the beginning, as their bodies are "starving" for real food and need time to adjust to the different ingredients and proportions in the recipe. Dr. Jean Hofve recommends feeding an adult cat as much as he or she will eat in twenty to thirty minutes, twice a day. Dr. Rob Silver recommends feeding one-half cup for each ten pounds of ideal body weight daily. Adjust as appropriate for your own cat's size, age, weight, and needs. Some cats may be dedicated nibblers. Encourage them to eat two meals per day, as recommended, but do not force them to be miserable.

Cats who have been fed dry food only may ignore and refuse to eat better foods. This simply means they are in even greater need! The pickier a cat is, the more addicted he probably is to his food. If cats have only eaten dry food or one type of wet food, they may not recognize the smell of raw or even cooked meat as food! Cats need to smell their food, and it needs to smell familiar and interesting. So, you must introduce homemade food very slowly. It can take months for a cat to fully accept it!

HOW TO INTRODUCE NEW FOOD

1 ↓ Start by feeding his usual commercial food twice a day only, leaving it down for one hour maximum. Do not leave food down between meals. (Tell your cat that you are making changes to his diet and eating schedule.)

2 ↓ Next, sprinkle a pinch of enzymes into or over the usual food at each meal for one week or so.

3 ↓ Introducing a better dry or canned food can help the cat feel better and help them accept changing to homemade eventually (see list of recommended foods in the resource section). Introduce new food gradually. In week one, mix one-quarter new food into three-quarters old food. In week two, give one-half to one-half. In week three, give three-quarters new to one-quarter old. And in week four, give all new food.

4 ↓ Once enzymes and better wet or dry foods have been accepted, take one-eighth teaspoon of the recipe and mix it thoroughly into the food. You can also cook a little extra ground meat and mix that in, or add water from a human grade can of tuna, a pinch of tuna, roast chicken, salmon—whatever your pets love.

5   If still feeding dry food, crush up some dry food.
↓   Make pea-sized meatballs with the recipe and roll in crushed dry food. Offer a few bites of the dry food, then remove and offer the meatballs.

6   If your cat still refuses, place a meatball in his mouth.
↓   Many people have had to do this for days until the cat finally decided he liked the new food!

7   Remind your cat that his old food will kill him or
↓   at least shorten his life. This new food is what his system needs to stay healthy and strong into old age! Don't give up! Your persistence will pay off in most cases. However, we have known cats who will refuse to the death to eat what's good for them. Sometimes an adopted cat (or dog) who experienced food shortages or starvation will become obsessed with their old food. They still carry a belief system in which they fear that there might not be a next meal. (See Part Two for help in changing this.)

Dr. Hofve reports that moldy grains routinely used in pet foods can cause "palatability depression" or "food aversion," resulting in the animal rejecting good food!

Do not fast a cat for more than twenty-four hours. This can result in liver damage or failure. If your cat is refusing to eat the new food, offer a little of the food they like. Once they have eaten some, remove it and offer the new food, perhaps mixed with the old. Be creative and cooperative. If this doesn't work, get help from a holistic vet or call us for support. Fortunately, dogs usually go for the good food. But if you have an exceptionally picky dog, try the preceding steps.

Remember, you and your family must commit to the diet change first. If you are not totally committed, your animal will sense that you are not and will simply wait until you give in and give him what he craves. Look at your own issues around food. Is feeding junk food a way to communicate love? Is destroying an animal's health by giving it too many treats a way to show love? Would you feed your children a diet of potato chips and soda alone just because they whine and beg for them? Is it better to make your loved ones happy in the moment or to create a foundation of health and happiness to sustain them over their entire lifetimes?

FRESH-FOOD RECIPE FOR DOGS

1 pound	Raw ground meat or poultry.
12 ounces	Puréed or chopped raw vegetables
8–10 ounces	Cooked grain
6–8 ounces	Purified water or chicken broth as needed
2 tablespoons	Oil
1 tablespoon	Food-grade bone meal with red marrow, or Dr. Silver's Calcium Balancing Powder (see recipe page 47), or a vitamin and mineral supplement with calcium, designed for dogs
Pinch	Canine enzyme supplement, sprinkled over food and mixed in just before serving

For dogs, the basic ingredients are 25–40 percent meat (protein + fat) and 60–75 percent veggies and grains. Visualize a rabbit, some crab apples, roots, and so on.

Mix all ingredients until you get the consistency of a thick chili. Add more purified water or broth as needed.

Once the basic recipe has been accepted, introduce a small amount of organic organ meats daily (one part organ to five parts muscle) or serve three times a week. Mix beef with beef-organ meats, lamb with lamb-organ meats, poultry with poultry-organ meats, and so on. Liver, kidneys, and heart must be from animals naturally raised on pesticide- and antibiotic-free feed since liver and kidneys are detoxing organs, and you don't want to pass toxins on to your dog. Cut organ meats into bite-sized chunks with a sharp knife or scissors.

You may include bribe foods such as cooked meats or favorite treats to entice your dog to eat. Dogs normally go for this new food rapidly, but if not, patiently persevere. This diet can mean a longer, healthier life; everything else is a compromise. It's okay in the beginning to cook the meat a little. Gradually cook it less and less until it's lightly seared and/or serve cooked meat mixed with raw if possible, and then add supplements and oils. Another option for chunks of meat is a quick dip in rapidly boiling water.

For vegetables, use raw zucchini, carrots, yellow squash, broccoli, green beans, peas, parsley—or cooked winter squash, yams, pumpkin, or other vegetables of your choice. Use one to three of these at a time and alternate. Leafy greens should be steamed if fed in large amounts due to competitive binding with calcium and iron. Garlic is great in small amounts, especially in the spring and summer to ward off biting insects. Don't use onions.

For grains, use oatmeal, barley flakes, rice, millet, quinoa, spelt, or rye, cooked to a gruel-like consistency. Use one grain at a time. Cooking grains in broth adds to the flavor. Grains may be eliminated entirely. Add more veggies; or substitute two four-ounce jars of organic baby-food vegetables or eight ounces of baked sweet potatoes mashed in a little butter for vegetables and grains.

For oil, use flaxseed, cod-liver, salmon, hempseed, or walnut oil, or a combination of two of these.

It's ideal to model ancestral eating habits, so leave food down no longer than forty-five minutes, morning and night. Offer food more frequently for puppies and pregnant or lactating dogs.

Food can be kept in the refrigerator for two to three days. Store in covered glass or plastic containers, or zip-lock bags. It's okay to prepare large quantities and freeze in serving portions. A zip-lock bag can hold one day's meals and be frozen in quantity.

Do not freeze meat more than twice, and try to refreeze within a few hours of mixing up the food. You may add supplements before freezing, but it's better to add them after defrosting. Enzymes must be added only at serving time. It's also better to add the delicate oils just before serving, as they can be compromised by freezing. It's always better to defrost in the refrigerator rather than leaving food to defrost on a counter, and never microwave anything! Microwave ovens disrupt and change cell activity in the food and possibly in the digestive tract as well. They transform the protein molecule shapes, altering nutritive value.

Most importantly, prepare and serve with love.

All of this may look complicated on the page, but once you prepare the recipe, you'll see how easy it is. If you'd like a demonstration, please see our videos. We show you step by step how to prepare each meal for your dog or cat. The results you'll see in your companion will show you that it's well worth the effort!

How much should you serve? A seventy-to-ninety-pound dog may need up to two pounds of food per day.[10] Dr. Silver recommends two to four cups for each twenty-five pounds of ideal body weight daily. Remember, substitute two cups of fresh food for one cup dry for a similar calorie count. Start with lesser amounts to judge your pet's needs, and do not overfeed. Be flexible, and feed your dog portions similar to what he is used to and then adjust as his body indicates. At first, he may behave as though he can't get enough. This is because his body is adjusting to real food. When proper nutrition is attained, dogs will usually self-regulate. If you have big dogs or a houseful of animals, you can add the recipe to an excellent dog kibble, such as those listed earlier in this chapter. This is far better than haphazardly adding vegetables, leftovers, or meat, which can actually cause potentially problematic imbalances in your dogs. Adding the recipe, which is fully balanced, to a well-balanced kibble will ensure optimal balance and health.

BONES AND CHUNKS OF MEAT

Once the basic recipe with organ meats has been fed for at least a week, start adding chunks of meat in place of some ground meat. Half and half is good. Raw, meaty bones are the final step. If your dog is eating raw ground meat, organ meat, and chunks of meat, start offering naturally raised, hormone- and antibiotic-free beef marrow bones or knuckle bones. If your dog has never eaten raw bones before, give him a large knuckle bone and watch him. Remove the bone after a half hour, put in a plastic bag, and refrigerate. You can repeat this for a couple of days until your dog learns to chew and eat bones slowly and carefully. Raw bones are the best thing for healthy teeth and gums.

Following is a handy chart to help you choose the ances-

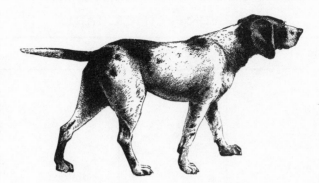

tral meats, vegetables, and grains for your dog. Remember to buy free-range, organic meat whenever possible, especially if you intend to feed raw. Fish should always be cooked unless you're willing and able to get "sushi-grade" fish. Organic veggies and grains will supply the best vitamins and minerals. A great source of information on breed-specific nutrition is William D. Cusick's *Canine Nutrition: Choosing the Best Food for Your Breed.* Cusick points out that each breed of dog comes from a specific part of the world and was raised for generations on local foods. Feeding your purebred dog a diet based on the foods their ancestors were raised on makes tremendous sense. A Chihuahua raised by the Aztecs in tropical Mexico has nutritional needs different from those of a Saint Bernard bred and raised in the Swiss Alps!

BREED-SPECIFIC CHART			
Breed of Dog	**Meats**	**Vegetables**	**Grains**

Beagle
  English
  American
Foxhound
Basset hound
Mountain Dog
  Bernese
  Greater Swiss
Great Pyrenees
Cocker Spaniel
Irish Setter
Papillon
Rottweiler
Saint Bernard
Terrier
   Scottish
   West Highland
	lamb alternated with rabbit, chicken	potatoes, parsley, carrots	oats, whole barley

Sheltie
Collie
Border Collie
Terrier
  Skye
  Norwich
  Welsh
Schipperke
Miniature Poodle
Pembroke Welsh Corgi
	cooked halibut, salmon, cod alternated with lamb, chicken	carrots, green beans, sweet potatoes, potatoes	oats, whole barley

Breed of Dog	Meats	Vegetables	Grains
Huskie Malamute Samoyed American Eskimo	fish, esp. salmon, cod, sardines, plus venison, elk, or buffalo	sweet potatoes	none
Greyhound Afghan Whippet Irish Wolfhound Scottish Deerhound Saluki Sloughi Lurcher	rabbit, chicken, turkey, venison	figs, apples, potatoes	brown rice, whole barley, bulgar wheat, oats
Chihuahua Bichon Frise Maltese	chicken, fish	avacado, figs	brown rice

Labrador
Golden Retriever
Retriever
   Chesapeake Bay
   Curly & Flat Coated
   Nova Scotia Duck Tolling
Newfoundland
Water Spaniel
   American
   Irish
Portugese Water Dog
Standard Poodle
	duck, chicken, fish – trout or salmon goose	potatoes, sweet potatoes, green beans, apples	occasionally oats or whole barley

Breed of Dog	Meats	Vegetables	Grains

German Shepherd
Doberman
Schnauzer
Great Dane
Dachshund
Terrier
    Yorkshire
    Norfolk
    Fox
    Staffordshire
English Bull
Neopolitan Mastiff
Pug
Airdale
Old English Sheepdog
Borzoi
	beef,
	lamb
		steamed cabbage,
		steamed collards,
		steamed cale
			oats,
			whole barley

Pekinese Japanese Chin Shih Tzu Chinese Crested Shiba Inu Akita Kyi Leo Japanese Spitz Lhasa Apso Tibetan Breeds	chicken, fish, lamb, occasional tofu	beets, green beans, steamed greens, bean sprouts	brown or white rice, millet

DR. SILVER'S CALCIUM BALANCING POWDER

If you wish to mix your own vitamin and mineral supplement, here is a recipe from Dr. Silver. He calls it "Calcium Balancing Powder" because it balances the calcium and phosphorus in the diet and adds a broad spectrum of whole food–bound vitamins and minerals.

1 part	Nutritional yeast
2 parts	Kelp powder
1 part	Lecithin granules
1 part	Bone meal

Always use food-grade ingredients from a health-food store. KAL and NOW vitamins are good brands of bone meal. You can substitute 700 mg. calcium lactate or gluconate, or one-third teaspoon eggshell powder for each teaspoon of bone meal. To make eggshell powder, bake eggshells at 450 degrees for forty-five minutes and then grind them. (1 teaspoon = 5 g.; 1 ounce = 30 g.; 1 cup = 240 g.) Refrigerate the mixture in an airtight container.

For dogs, give one to two teaspoons of the Calcium Balancing Powder per fifteen pounds of body weight daily. For cats, give one-quarter to one-half teaspoon daily. Use this mixture instead of the one tablespoon of bone meal in the fresh-food recipes.

Dr. Silver recommends flaxseed, hempseed, walnut, and fish oils as the best sources of essential fatty acids. These oils can be alternated or can be mixed. They provide healthy omega-3, 6 and 9 fatty acids and valuable vitamins. They should be used in conjunction with the Calcium Balancing Powder. Add 100 IU of Vitamin E for cats and small dogs, 200 IU for medium (thirty-to-sixty-pound) dogs, and 400 IU for large dogs. Vitamin E is a powerful antioxidant. Keep oils refrigerated.

For dogs, give one teaspoon oil per fifteen pounds of body weight daily. Do not exceed one tablespoon per day unless otherwise instructed. For cats, give one-quarter to one-half teaspoon daily.

Include an enzyme supplement with lactobacillus acidophilus. Plain yogurt with active cultures is highly beneficial for dogs and cats. Yogurt is a simple, inexpensive way to add a powerful digestive aid with immune system supporting bacteria to your animal's life. Yogurt also helps rebuild the beneficial bacteria destroyed by antibiotics. Yogurt supplies moisture and calcium as well. Offer your animal one teaspoon (small dog or cat) to one-half cup (large dog) of yogurt with or before each meal.

Remember to leave food down for an hour maximum.

Free-feeding is not good for a predator's system. Refrigerate leftovers. For the next meal,
warm leftovers to room temperature with
warm water and add more enzymes. Uneaten
raw meat should be thrown away after the second
meal, or sooner in warm weather. Use common
sense; if any food smells spoiled, throw it away.
Fresh, filtered water should always be available.
(Water from toilets does not fall into this category.)
We know of one cat whose chronic cystitis cleared
up when her owner switched from tap to filtered
water. If your cat or dog has had any kidney difficulties, dis-
tilled water should be offered. Use ceramic or glass bowls
for both food and water, and wash them regularly with hot,
soapy water. Plastic bowls hold bacteria, and stainless-steel
bowls can hold an electromagnetic charge. Again, do not
use a microwave.

If you are concerned that giving your animal "people
food" will turn him or her into a beggar, understand that
animals beg for two reasons:

1. They are desperate for fresh, unprocessed, real
   food.

2. We teach them that it is OK to beg when we feed
   them at the table or while we are preparing food.

Normally, if an animal is begging out of need, better
food and proper nutrition will eliminate the problem. If
an animal is begging out of habit, you and she both need
behavior modification!

HEALTHY HORSE FEED

1. Feed a variety of grasses scattered on the ground
   or at least lower than chest height.

2. Make diet changes gently and gradually.

3. Provide plenty of clean, filtered water.

The average one-thousand-pound horse requires twenty-five gallons of water per day.[11] And remember, horses are grazers. Unlike cats and dogs, horses are built to eat on and off all day long—not twice a day. They require a variety of fresh grasses, such as Timothy, Rye, Bermuda, Orchard, and Brome. Horses can handle a little grain and alfalfa. However, feeding too much grain and alfalfa can lead to intestinal stones and contribute to Cushings disease and chronic laminitis. Find organic feed, as most horse feed can be laden with pesticides. Ground flaxseed added to a horse's diet will support a healthy immune system, enhance absorption of nutrients, particularly minerals, and supply essential Omega-3 fatty acids. Probiotics can also aid digestion and absorption. They are especially valuable to foals, older horses, and any horse prone to colic and digestive upsets. See resource section for suppliers.

Bach Flower Remedies
for Balanced Emotions

CHAPTER 4

A Little Historical Background

The only true healing is reminding a being of perfect health

and balance. Anything else is invasive.

— Cat

Now that we have discussed how to help animals be balanced physically, through proper nutrition, it is important to look at ways to support their emotional balance. There is an extraordinary, inexpensive, and very effective tool available for helping an animal to prepare for change, surgery, or travel, as well as to deal with and recover from abuse, neglect, physical and emotional trauma, abandonment, fear, shyness, and aberrational behaviors. This tool is the collection of flower remedies developed by Dr. Edward Bach, M.D.

The Bach Flower Remedies were originally developed for human beings, but have been found to work beautifully with animals as well. Dr. Bach (pronounced "batch") was a Welsh physician who practiced in England in the late 1920s. He began to be discouraged when some of his patients were unable to heal. Looking at these individuals, he noticed that each of them had a major emotional issue, problem, or trauma. He began to believe that the only way to heal these patients physically was to find a way to first heal them emotionally. Conventional medicine offered few satisfactory tools. He stopped practicing medicine and devoted himself to research. He began by thinking about plants and trees, noting how most medications were derived from plant sources. He thought that perhaps the energy of the plants and trees could affect the energy of the human patient. Working with the plants and trees in his own garden and the surrounding countryside, he clairvoyantly matched the symptoms of human emotional imbalances with plant partners to help in the healing. For example, he found that the holly tree could help heal jealousy and a bad temper. Dr. Bach "harnessed" the healing energy of the plants and trees by picking blossoms and soaking them for hours in purified water in the sunshine. This process infused the energy from the blossoms into the water. He then diluted the essence-filled water, put it in small-dosage bottles, and preserved each bottle with brandy.

Working with the flowers of the local plants and trees in this way, Dr. Bach developed thirty-eight individual remedies and one combination remedy for emergencies, which he called "Rescue Remedy."

Dr. Bach began testing these "flower remedies" on himself first and then on his human patients. The results were miraculous. Childhood traumas, anger, jealousy, depression, fear, lack of confidence, impatience, intolerance, abusive behavior, possessiveness—all began to come into balance and be healed. At last, the patients were ready to heal on a physical level.

How do the Bach Flower Remedies work? They are similar to homeopathic remedies. It is believed that they, like homeopathic remedies, work on the energy body or aura of a person or animal. This is the nonphysical part of us just outside or around our physical bodies. This energy body, called the "physical etheric," is where an imbalance or illness often occurs before manifesting in the physical body. Dr. Bach believed that to treat the imbalance in the physical etheric was to effect a more permanent cure in the physical body. Somehow the energetic qualities of the flowers help to harmonize people and animals toward emotional and physical balance. For more than sixty years, countless people and animals have been helped by these Bach Flower Remedies when drugs and conventional therapies could do little or nothing to bring them into emotional health.

How do you find the "right" remedy? The next section
of this chapter contains a summary of the remedies as they
apply to animals. Dr. Dee Blanco introduced me to the Bach
Flower Remedies. Dr. Joann Stefanatos and Dr. Jean Hofve
added their experience to ours. We hope you will find this
information helpful for you and your animals. To read more
on the Bach Flower Remedies for human beings, consult
your local library or bookstore for the many available books
on the subject.

Writing for the *Journal of the American Holistic Veterinary
Medical Association,* Dr. Stefanatos stated to her veterinary
colleagues:

> Remember that animals have an emotional body as well as
> a physical body. The Bach Flowers resonate with the emo-
> tional body to reestablish equilibrium and harmony in the
> body (physical). The emotional status of an animal deter-
> mines how quickly its body will heal. A change in energy
> must occur before there is a change in physical structure.
> Thusly, a change of energy occurs in the Aura of an animal
> before symptoms are manifested physically. Any disequi-
> librium occurring in the mental body will lead to the symp-
> toms animals are presented within our daily practices.
>
> Because Bach Flower Remedies can be used in humans and
> animals to treat the 'whole body,' they should be the first

homeopathic to introduce to fellow conventional practitioners who just want to see how well homeopathy works.[12]

Many veterinary clinics, shelters, rescuers, trainers, and
individuals use the Bach Flower Remedies for animals. Dr.
Hofve, formerly of the South Penn Cat Clinic in Denver,
sprayed Rescue Remedy in the examination room between
patients. She saw a huge difference in the cats when she did
this. They were calmer, more relaxed, and more cooperative. The Cat Care Society in Lakewood, Colorado, kept all
thirty-nine remedies ready to be mixed for the strays and
rescued cats who arrive for their care. They will often send
cats to their new homes with a remedy mixture designed
to ease the transition and help the cats adjust to their new
homes and families. Dr. Blanco of Santa Fe, New Mexico,
uses the Bach Flower Remedies to support many healing
therapies she prescribes. Other vets report fewer complications from surgeries and shorter recovery times for animals
on the flower remedies. Horse trainer Karen Whitman
has used them for years with her own and her clients'
horses and has seen remarkable changes in the animals.
With the help of the flower remedies, the horses are able
to release old memories, stuck patterns, and fears. She has

found increased attention spans, better concentration, and improved retention of new lessons. Barbara Ludt, a long-time rescuer of ferrets and other animals in Florida and Washington, uses the flower remedies to aid in recovery as well as to support dying animals. They are an extremely valuable tool for her in rehabilitating "fear biters."

If all shelters, animal-control officers, and rescuers used Rescue Remedy regularly, they would find a marked difference in animals. Dogs respond with less fear and aggression; feral cats become calmer and easier to handle; injured animals become more cooperative and less panicked. Rescue Remedy is a miracle all by itself!

Flower remedies are not aromatherapy. Flower essences have no scent and are derived from the energy of the plant. Flower essences are completely safe, but aromatherapy essential oils are potent medicine, which can be dangerous if misused. Do not confuse the flower essences described in this handbook with essential oils. Essential oils must be used with extreme caution and with the guidance of qualified practioners.

CHAPTER 5

The Bach Flower Remedies for Animals

Remember, it is we who nourish your bodies and help you come into balance.

— PLANTS

Each flower remedy listed below is created from the blossom of a flowering tree or plant, except for Rock Water. (Rock Water remedy is created from stream water where it flows over rocks.) Today, all the Bach Flower Remedies are created under strict supervision, according to Dr. Bach's specifications. They are available individually and in full sets in health-food shops and holistic pet stores all over the world. See the resources for some mail-order outlets.

AGRIMONY

For animals who never complain, even when they are obviously in pain.

For animals who chew themselves raw due to any form of skin irritation—for instance, from food allergies, pollens, or grass intolerance.

For animals who are irritated by sutures and constantly lick their wounds.

For animals who are tormented by biting ticks, fleas, or parasites.

For animals who are restless and search from place to place but cannot quite get comfortable, and once comfortable, are up again and unable to settle in.

For animals who pace back and forth, especially wild animals who are unable to adjust to captivity.

The key word for Agrimony is *tolerance*.

ASPEN

For animals who spook very easily.

For animals who feel separate and afraid and need to reconnect.

For animals who sense impending harm before and during intense storms, thunder, tornadoes, flooding, earthquakes, and so on.

For animals who are in shelters, sense that other animals have been put to death, and experience the apprehension that they are next, like the fear that cattle experience before slaughter.

The key word for Aspen is *connection*.

❧ BEECH ❧

For animals, especially cats, who are picky eaters or usually refuse food.

For animals who bark, squawk, whine, or complain all the time.

For animals who have intolerance to or irritations from grasses.

For animals who have intolerance to heat, humidity, or cold.

For animals who have intolerance toward children or other animals, especially older animals who have to tolerate a puppy or kitten.

For animals who do not want to tolerate new relationships in their houses:

> Cats who spray on the belongings of their person's newfound mate.
>
> Dogs who attack or growl at their person's new mate.
>
> Birds who peck the "intruder," displaying their dislike.
>
> Horses who act up when mounted by someone other than their usual rider-person.
>
> The key word for Beech is *acceptance.*

❧ CENTAURY ❧

For animals who do not stand up for themselves and allow other animals to push them around:

> Horses in corrals.
>
> Birds in cages.
>
> Cats abused by dogs or vice versa.

For animals who are overly attentive and loyal, and want to please their person at all costs.

For animals who need to increase their will to live, especially when fighting an illness, after an accident, or even during a very hard birth and delivery.

The key word for Centaury is *positive*.

❧ CERATO ❧

For animals who need certainty, steadiness, and strength.

For animals who are mentally flighty and inattentive.

For animals who are easily distracted and need to be able to better listen to and concentrate on their person's commands during training and competitive show events.

The key word for Cerato is *certainty*.

❧ CHERRY PLUM ❧

For animals who lose control, become crazed and wild, and are destructive and tear up their houses or yards:

> Vicious animals who become dangerous when provoked.

> High-strung animals, including horses.

> Animals (of both sexes) during mating season.

For animals who need to remain in control:

> In competition, when stressed by strange people, noises, gunfire, and other animals.

> When seeing other animals enter into their territory.

For animals who become frantic when traveling:

> Cats when traveling in cars.

> Horses who spook while being placed in trailers.

> All animals when flying.

For animals who suffer from seizures, anxiety attacks, loss of control of bodily functions such as bladder control, and possible dysplastic conditions.

For animals who chew themselves, chase their own tails uncontrollably, have allergies to grasses, or need to stay away from stitches after surgery.

Cherry Plum helps an animal make good choices.

> The key word for Cherry Plum is *self-control*.

Note: Cherry Plum is one of the five remedies in Rescue Remedy.

CHESTNUT BUD

For animals who need to break bad habits:

> Dogs who chew shoes, get into the trash, etcetera.
>
> Dogs who run fences, chase horses, cars, etcetera.
>
> Dogs who eat eggs or chickens.
>
> Horses who won't leave corrals.
>
> Dogs who jump up on everyone.

For animals who have a difficult time learning.

For animals who need to increase rapid learning, memory, and retention of new lessons during training sessions.

For working dogs and horses who need to increase a keen sense of awareness.

> The key word for Chestnut Bud is *attentiveness*.

CHICORY

For animals who think that they own their person and house:

> Dogs or cats who demand to be fed.

Animals who demand all the attention.

For animals who are overly possessive:

> Females with their litters, especially when it is time for the young to leave the nest.

> Dogs on guard against anyone harming family members, especially children.

> Birds who are very possessive of a sole owner-person.

> Mothers who are overpreening or overattentive in the care of their young.

For animals who are emotionally unable to let go of a person or an animal mate to whom they were very attached.

For animals who show signs of physical congestion in lungs or nasal passages. (This congestion could be a sign of a need for more attention. Evaluate whether you have been ignoring the animal.)

The key word for Chicory is *unconditional*.

❧ CLEMATIS ❧

For animals who need to increase attention span and the ability to focus on
training lessons at hand:

> Guard dogs.

> Hunting dogs.

> Seeing-eye dogs.

For animals who are comatose or unconscious.

For animals who have had surgery and need to speed recovery and increase alertness.

The key word for Clematis is *conscious*.

Note: Clematis is one of the five remedies in Rescue Remedy.

❧ CRAB APPLE ❧

For animals who need to be rid of odor:

> Dogs who have been caught by skunks.

> Dogs who have rolled in manure or garbage.

For animals who have had an infestation of lice, fleas, ticks, or any form of parasite, including worms, and need to alleviate their unclean feelings.

For animals who need to cleanse toxic material from their systems due to poisons of any kind, including insect-spray poisoning, chemicals, and contaminated food or water.

For animals who have infectious or open wounds or rashes of any kind.

For animals who are extremely distraught and need to flush out emotional toxins:

> Animals who have been abandoned and left to die.

> Animals who have been abused.

For animals who need to detoxify after colds or viral or bacterial infections.

For animals who have a poor self-image:

> Animals who don't hold their heads high during competitions.

> Animals who cower and hide.

> Animals who have had their coats cut or shaved.

The key word for Crab Apple is *cleansing*.

❧ ELM ❧

For animals who are overwhelmed by situations, such as flying, leaving home, or changing locations, having too many visitors, or going to be groomed:

> Birds who become easily overwhelmed and frazzled with children (and often men in general), or when their wings, nails, and bills need trimming.

> Horses being shod.

For animals who are naturally high-strung and easily overwhelmed, even by everyday events:

> Race horses.

> Show dogs and cats.

The key word for Elm is *adaptable*.

❧ GENTIAN ❧

For animals who have suffered setbacks of any kind.

For animals who worsen or seem discouraged in long illnesses:

> With arthritis-type symptoms.

> Rehabilitating from surgery.

> Disappointed when babies are born dead.

For animals who are not confident and lack faith in their ability to conquer what has been set before them:

> Horses expected to perform difficult exercises or endurance rides.

> Sled dogs expected to display extreme physical endurance.

The key word for Gentian is *hopeful*.

❧ GORSE ❦

For animals who show signs of giving up or feeling that their condition is hopeless, such as refusing to eat or to improve:

With cancer.

With arthritis-type complications.

With a critical injury or after surgery.

The key word for Gorse is *vibrant*.

❧ HEATHER ❦

For animals who have to be the centers of attention.

For animals who engage in mischievous adventures like tearing up the house in order to receive attention.

For animals who annoy and pester family or company.

For animals who always want to sleep in your bed or sit in the middle of your lap, even when you are busy.

For animals who do not respond well when left alone, possibly expressing loneliness or a feeling of being unloved.

For animals who are in a kennel away from their person, and especially animals in shelters who receive no attention.

The key word for Heather is *satisfied*.

❧ HOLLY ❦

For animals who show signs of jealousy or have a temper:

Birds who have a tendency to bite or anger easily.

Dogs or horses known to be vicious and dangerous.

Animals who have been captured or injured.

For animals who need more love:

>   Abused animals.

>   Neglected animals.

>   Horses who are never ridden, shod, or properly fed.

>   Dogs left outside and chained.

For animals who must endure torturous quarantine, especially birds.

>   The key word for Holly is *loved*.

>   ## HONEYSUCKLE

For animals who need support after a loved person or a dear friend has passed on or been taken away:

>   Animals who mate for life.

>   Race animals who sulk and somehow have given up the desire to win.

For animals who need to replenish depleted energies:

>   Horses who have been exhausted or overexerted.

>   Sled dogs who become exhausted.

>   Any animals chased to exhaustion.

>   Mothers exhausted after long birthing ordeals, especially when having to nurse and care for young while recuperating from the birth or other extenuating circumstances.

>   Any animals who have lost too much blood or when vital energies are low.

For animals who are homesick when being sold or given away, placed in a kennel, or having to remain hospitalized at the vet.

>   The key word for Honeysuckle is *full*.

HORNBEAM

For animals who are weary in body or spirit.

For animals who are tired after competition.

For animals who have lost the will to compete, win, or do their jobs.

The key word for Hornbeam is *energy*.

IMPATIENS

For animals who have any form of nervous difficulties, especially nervous shakes.

For animals who are overly anxious at feeding times or before races.

For animals who have convulsions or epileptic fits, especially when agitated by being overly excited or upset.

For animals who have any form of pain.

The key word for Impatiens is *patience*.

Note: Impatiens is one of the five remedies in Rescue Remedy.

LARCH

For animals who need increased confidence and self-esteem during competitive events so that they hold their heads high and enjoy themselves.

For animals who have no confidence, or sense of safety or security.

For animals who cower easily or hide.

For animals who have been beaten and abused, causing

confusion, a lack of confidence, and the need to restore "the rug that was pulled out from under them."

The key word for Larch is *confidence*.

❧ MIMULUS ❧

For animals who suffer from long-term fears:

Of being abused.

Of being starved.

Of strangers.

Of men.

Of lightning and thunder.

Of other animals.

Of abandonment.

For animals who are easily dominated by other animals, do not fight for themselves, and do not assume their rightful places.

For animals who have illnesses that do not respond to treatment.

The key word for Mimulus is *fearless*.

❧ MUSTARD ❧

For animals who experience very deep depressions, especially when complicated by hormonal changes.

For animals who are pregnant, especially if any unusual depression or abnormal behavior is observed.

For animals who become very cantankerous when in season.

For animals who like to be alone and become obnoxious and cranky when approached, especially older animals.

The key word for Mustard is *happy*.

OAK

For animals who are hard workers yet seem to be overburdened and struggle with tasks at hand:

> Swayback horses whose over-service is observable by stress in the back.

> Animals stressed by arthritis-type symptoms, who struggle just to move about or to rise after resting for any length of time.

> Mothers in the last months of long pregnancies or during exceptionally long deliveries.

For animals who have begun to struggle with long chronic illnesses.

For animals who need strength when subjected to harsh living conditions such as cold, heat, or lack of food:

> Animals who have been starved for any length of time and need to rebuild strength.

> Domesticated or wild animals who have endured long, cold winters.

For animals who never complain, many times taking on more responsibility than others:

> Sled dogs or working dogs before long runs.

> Horses ridden extensively or worked hard.

For animals whose most prominent virtue is to remain strong in character.

The key word for Oak is *strength*.

❧ OLIVE ❧

For animals who suffer exhaustion from especially long ordeals or from long-term pain:

> Elderly animals who easily become exhausted.
>
> Animals plagued with allergies, causing their adrenals to be stressed.

Wild animals who are caged and who have exhausted themselves by trying to escape or constantly running in their cages.

The key word for Olive is *endurance*.

❧ PINE ❧

For animals who have been abused and feel rejected:

> Animals who have been given away or left behind.
>
> Rescued animals from shelters, humane societies, or pounds.
>
> Unlucky animals who never seem to win yet are quite capable of doing so.

For animals who act guilty whenever their person is upset, even though their person's emotions are not directed toward them.

The key word for Pine is *security*.

❧ RED CHESTNUT ❧

For animals who constantly look out windows, worrying about their person or animal friends.

For animals who are overly concerned about their young.

The key word for Red Chestnut is *trust*.

ROCK ROSE

For animals who feel terror and panic after an accident, injury, fire, or any other terrifying event.

For animals who are overly fearful (and were possibly terrified once) and whose old fears do not dissolve away naturally.

For animals who are used in service, such as police, rescue, and emergency work, to accentuate their already innate abilities and dauntless courage.

The key word for Rock Rose is *courage*.

Note: Rock Rose is one of the five remedies in Rescue Remedy.

ROCK WATER

For animals who have become stiff in their joints and muscles and need to increase flexibility.

For animals who are uncompromising, picky eaters, and are inflexible in their eating habits.

The key word for Rock Water is *flexibility*.

SCLERANTHUS

For animals who need to restore balance:

> With equilibrium difficulties.
>
> With neurological confusion, such as might happen with some kinds of seizures.
>
> Who have had strokes or are partially paralyzed.
>
> Who are accused of being clumsy.
>
> With hormonal fluctuations that cause behavioral problems (such as mood swings) or physical problems (such as motion sickness).

The key word for Scleranthus is *balance*.

STAR OF BETHLEHEM

For animals who need to heal and release any form of trauma:

Emotional trauma from the loss of a loved person or mate, especially those animals who mate for life.

Physical trauma after injuries of any kind, including abuse or auto accidents.

Birthing trauma.

Trauma from extreme cold or heat.

For animals who need to receive comfort:

Animals left alone or in kennels, and that feel unloved.

Injured or ill animals who must remain at veterinary clinics.

The key word for Star of Bethlehem is *comfort*.

Note: Star of Bethlehem is one of the five remedies in Rescue Remedy.

SWEET CHESTNUT

For animals who are at their wits' ends from being forced to remain in very close quarters, such as small kennels or small rooms.

For animals who are very high-strung.

For animals who need to prevent "burnout," especially animals who race or show.

For animals who need endurance energy, such as for competition races.

The key word for Sweet Chestnut is *freedom*.

❧ VERVAIN ☙

For animals who are very intense, hyperactive, and high-strung:

> Dogs who run fences.
>
> Dogs who chase cars.
>
> Horses who pace their corrals or chew their stalls nervously.
>
> Dogs who will not quit barking.

The key word for Vervain is *calmness*.

❧ VINE ☙

For animals who think they are in charge of their houses.

For animals who rule any other animals, obviously the boss or wishing to be.

For animals who need support during competitive events to instill leadership.

The key word for Vine is *respect*.

❧ WALNUT ☙

For animals who need to stabilize and adjust to new surroundings:

> Moving to new homes across the city or country.
>
> Adjusting to new people.
>
> Adjusting to traveling; planes, cars, boats, etcetera.

For animals who need protection from outside influences:

> Insecticides, pollutants, sensitivities to pollens and grasses.
>
> Sensitivities to thunderstorms or loud noises.
>
> Sensitivities to their person's difficulties or illnesses.

For animals who need to provide and support healthy boundaries for themselves.

The key word for Walnut is *stability*.

WATER VIOLET

For animals who never complain and who, when sick, prefer to be left alone to heal themselves.

For animals who feel grief when their person or mate dies, or when they are forced to be parted.

For animals who prefer to be alone and quiet, but don't seem totally happy about it.

The key word for Water Violet is *tranquillity*.

WHITE CHESTNUT

For animals who need clear, uninterrupted focus and concentration, such as horses and dogs in competition.

For animals who need to support quiet, calm minds.

The key word for White Chestnut is *clarity*.

WILD OAT

For animals who were bred or trained for specific purposes but are not being used for those.

For animals who are bored and feeling useless, especially animals who chew up or destroy things because they are bored.

For animals who need a sense of usefulness and purpose.

For animals who need to have their interests rekindled.

The key word for Wild Oat is *determination*.

❧ WILD ROSE ☙

For animals who need help remaining happy and content:

> Dogs chained up or forced to remain in small areas.
>
> Older animals forced to keep company with younger, more annoying animals.
>
> Old, grouchy, or cantankerous animals, including birds.

For animals who need to return joy to any situations or relationships.

The key word for Wild Rose is *joy*.

❧ WILLOW ☙

For animals who show resentment:

> Cats who urinate in inappropriate places because of something you did to them.
>
> Dogs who chew up the entire house because you left them alone all day.

Animals who ignore you because you left them all day or placed them in a kennel.

The key word for Willow is *optimism*.

❧ RESCUE REMEDY ☙

For animals who need an emergency or first-aid formula for stress, shock, injury, fear, and/or exhaustion. It is used for support through any challenge—physical, emotional, or spiritual—and to restore a sense of safety, peace, and calm.

Rescue Remedy is made up of:

- Cherry Plum—to help retain control.

- Clematis—to restore consciousness.

- Impatiens—to relieve pain and anxiety.

- Rock Rose—to relieve panic and fear.

- Star of Bethlehem—to comfort and to release trauma.

The following chart lists the positive qualities we wish to support in our animals.

BACH FLOWER CHART	
QUALITY	**BACH FLOWERS**
Acceptance	Agrimony, Beech, Willow, Wild Rose
Adaptability	Elm, Beech, Impatiens, Scleranthus
Balance	Century, Scleranthus, Vervain, Walnut
Calm	Cherry Plum, Mustard, Red Chestnut, Water Violet
Clarity & Focus	Chestnut Bud, Clematis, Heather, White Chestnut
Cleansing & Release	Crab Apple, Impatiens, Star of Bethlehem
Comfort & Safety	Star of Bethlehem, Larch, Walnut, Red Chestnut
Confidence	Larch, Aspen, Cerato, Mimulus, Pine, Rock Rose
Dependability	Gentian, Oak
Flexibility	Rock Water, Sweet Chestnut, Wild Rose, Willow
Generosity	Chicory, Holly, Beech
Hopefulness	Honeysuckle, Gentian
Joyfulness	Rock Water, Wild Rose
Understanding	Sweet Chestnut, Vine, Wild Oat
Vitality	Hornbeam, Gentian, Gorse, Olive
	TO BE USED FOR EMERGENCIES:
	Rescue Remedy, Cherry Plum, Clematis, Impatiens, Rock Rose, Star of Bethlehem

BACH FLOWERS FOR PLANTS

The same Bach Flower Remedies you use for your animals are great for the garden, too. Spray diluted remedies on affected areas and add a few drops to the watering mixture until health and balance are restored.

ASPEN relieves the apprehension plants and trees feel when their surroundings are being destroyed by the machines of mankind.

CENTURY supports balance and strength in plants that have feeble-looking limbs, seemingly lacking the will to live, especially when surrounding plants easily crowd them out of their space and light.

CLEMATIS re-energizes plants that have been dormant during the winter or that appear to be dead.

CRAB APPLE is a cleansing remedy for plants that have fungus or mold, and/or feel unclean. Use any time there is an environmental contamination. Use Crab Apple for cleaning contaminants and pesticides from fruits and vegetables.

ELM calms and revitalizes plants that have been stressed by too much water, dryness, heat, or cold, or abuse by dogs, cats, or children.

HOLLY supports plants that have been neglected and require more love and attention.

MIMULUS gives energy to plants with diseases that are difficult to cure. (May be used to save an entire crop from ruin if caught early enough.)

Oak strengthens all plants that have to struggle for life when growing in harsh environments, especially trees needing to grow stronger trunks.

Star of Bethlehem comforts plants that have endured traumas from the elements or injury.

Sweet Chestnut supplies energy to plants that are dying, seemingly at their wits' ends.

Walnut protects plants from environmental pollutants and contaminants, and helps them adjust to temperature or location changes.

Wild Rose gives hope to plants that have lost their zeal for life.

Rescue Remedy can also help any plant or tree that has recently experienced trauma from fire, pesticides, storms, etc.

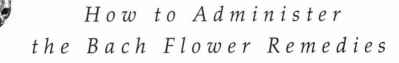

CHAPTER 6

How to Administer the Bach Flower Remedies

Health is balance on all levels—physical, emotional, mental and spiritual. All are intertwined and inseparable.

— CAT

Many good health-food stores and holistic pet shops carry the Bach Flower Remedies (in either premixed or "stock" form) or can order them for you. They are available in full sets or in individual one-ounce dropper bottles. If you are planning to mix them yourself, you will need to buy a one-ounce glass dropper bottle as well, and consult the next section of this chapter for instructions. If you cannot find the remedies locally, see the resources for shops.

HOW TO CHOOSE THE BACH FLOWER REMEDIES

1. Identify your animal's issue. Write down a positive mission statement. (See the chart at the end of this chapter.) For example, if you wish to help two animals who are fighting, state something like:

   "I ask for those remedies that will restore friendship and harmony between Mike and Jeff."

2. Read the descriptions of each remedy. Which remedies jump out at you?

3. Make a list of all remedies that seem to apply to your animal.

4. Prioritize them.

5. Choose the top four to seven.

6. If you are having a specific difficulty, such as two animals who are fighting, choose those remedies that calm and restore peace and security. Give both animals the same remedy.

7. Ask your animal's higher self which remedies are best for a particular situation.

8. If you need to "sleep on it," ask the healing angels, your guides and helpers, and your animal to choose the best remedies for the situation.

9. If you are unable to get your own answers, call us for a consultation to ask your animal which remedies are best for him or her.

Some examples of this process follow.

Your rescued cat is needy and clingy when alone with you, but around other people she is shy and fearful. She has had at least two homes before yours and is a picky eater. Let's find the positive opposites of her symptoms and focus on these while choosing remedies:

NEGATIVE SYMPTOM	POSITIVE QUALITY	FLOWER REMEDY
Needy, clingy	Autonomous, selfless	Heather, Chicory
Shy, fearful, loner	Outgoing, courageous	Mimulus, Water Violet
Unstable	Stable, self-confident	Larch
Picky	Accepting, flexible	Rock Water, Beech

Another way to work with the flower remedies is to focus on the situation as well as on the individual:

You are planning a trip and want to create a remedy to support your animals while you are away. You want them to handle the change in the routine, be happy, behave normally, and be worry-free and content with the house-sitter.

POSITIVE QUALITY	FLOWER REMEDY
Able to handle change	Walnut, Elm
Happy, content	Wild Rose
Worry-free	Red Chestnut
Accepting of the house-sitter	Beech

And if one of your animals starts to chew his paw or the leg of your favorite chair whenever you're away, you could include Agrimony and Cherry Plum.

You are bringing home a new puppy and want your

older animals to accept her. You want to help everybody
adjust to the change and accept each other. You want to help
the puppy let go of her mother and original home and be
happy with you and your family in your home:

POSITIVE QUALITY	FLOWER REMEDY
Acceptance, adjustment	Beech, Wild Rose
Confidence, being present	Larch, Honeysuckle
Coping well with change	Elm, Walnut

And if travel or separation might be stressful or traumatic, Rescue Remedy would make sense.

In this situation, ideally you would begin to administer
a mixture to your animals three to four days before the
puppy arrives and ask the breeder to give the puppy the
same mixture during the same period. By administering
the remedy before all the animals are brought together, you
help align their energies to each other and provide a positive, nurturing, energetic environment for everybody. If you
can't give the animals the remedy before the puppy arrives,
begin as soon as possible. Typically, when flower remedies
are used to help a new animal make a transition into a new
home, the adjustment time is cut considerably. All involved,

humans and animals, have a much greater chance of getting off to a better start than without the remedies.

HOW TO MIX THE BACH FLOWER REMEDIES

If you choose to buy and mix the remedies yourself, you
will need:

- The individual bottled remedies (stock bottles)
- A one- or two-ounce sterile, brown or blue glass dropper bottle
- White vinegar or glycerine
- Filtered water
- Labels

Fill the glass bottle three-quarters full with filtered
water. Place two to four drops from each stock bottle that
you are using in the mixture into the glass bottle. Add
one-quarter dropper full of white vinegar or glycerine as
a preservative. Top off with filtered water. Label the bottle
with the animal's name, the date, and the positive goal. For
example: "for peace, harmony, and trust." Store in a cool,
dry place.

If you notice particles or mold developing in the bottle,
pour out mixture, boil the bottle and dropper five to ten
minutes to sterilize them, and start over.

HOW TO ADMINISTER THE BACH FLOWER REMEDIES

Shake the bottle, tapping firmly against the heel of your hand ten times each time before administering. This energizes the mixture. From this bottle, you can:

1. Give two to four drops directly into the animal's mouth. Be careful not to let them lick the dropper. If they do, rinse the dropper under hot tap water for a few minutes before replacing it in the bottle.

2. Add two to four drops to food or water.

3. Add four drops to filtered water in a small spray bottle and spray the room, bedding, favorite chair, crate, car, etcetera.

4. Place a few drops on your own hands and pet your animal's head and ears.

5. Combine several or all of the above methods.

6. It is very important that each time you administer, you tell your animal what the remedy is for, using only positive statements.

If using a remedy straight from the stock bottle, notice that it is preserved with quite a bit of brandy. For birds, fish, repiles, and sensitive animals, boil off the brandy before administering. To do this, boil about one-quarter to one-half cup water and pour it into a Pyrex measuring cup. Add two to four drops of the stock remedy to the water. Leave it for a moment. The alcohol will boil off. When the water has cooled, pour it into a brown glass dropper bottle, label, and use.

The remedies are not medications and do not have to be swallowed. They simply need to make contact with the animal's mucous membranes or enter into their energy field to be effective. Two to four drops is the amount needed by either a canary or a horse, as Bach Flower Remedies are not medicines.

In an emergency, one to two drops of Rescue Remedy can be administered every two to ten minutes until emergency medical help arrives or you arrive at the emergency clinic. It can be placed on the lips of an unconscious animal or rubbed on the ears. If you are in an emergency situation with your animal, you can take a few drops yourself to help you cope and make clearheaded decisions. It is always worthwhile to carry a bottle with you in case of an unexpected need.

For most behavioral or emotional problems, start with two to four drops, two to three times per day for two to four weeks. Once improvement is established, you can wean the animal by dropping back to once a day, then every other day, and so on. Some animals need to be on the remedies longer. Others will need to return to the remedies briefly during times of stress or change. In cases where the problem is mild—or where the situation is acute, such as an operation—you may only need to give the drops a few times. In situations when you can "catch him in the act," administer immediately, reinforcing the message by telling him that the remedy is to help him pee in the correct place, chew the correct toy, behave gently with the puppy, and so on. Your positive reinforcement and intention will help ensure success.

If you are giving remedies to one animal in a multi-animal household, never fear. The remedies can go into the shared water bowl. If the other animals need help from any remedy in the mixture, they will receive it. If not, the remedies will have no effect whatsoever. The Bach Flower Remedies either help or they don't. There are no side effects or negative interactions with other therapies or medications. Sometimes, in the process of releasing emotions, your animal may have a strong reaction. The flower remedies work to replace a negative emotional state with a positive one, but sometimes this means that the animal may have to act out to release and heal. Normally this happens for a brief time. In rare cases where a reaction occurs, support your animal by allowing him to express himself without punishment, or give him privacy to work through the emotions. Both of you will be better for this. If you find this stressful, consider taking a few drops of the remedy yourself. Odds are good that the remedy you have created for your animal can help you just as much.

Animals are often mirrors of stresses and strains in our lives. They often act out to get our attention and to help us see our own imbalances. Animals also "take on" illness and disease to help us. If you can step out of the purely physical situation and ask yourself what your animal may be trying to tell you by manifesting an emotional or physical problem, you could learn a great deal about yourself. Taking flower remedies with our animals and being willing to heal ourselves on every level may do more to help our animals heal than any therapy or medication can. At the very least, spraying the remedies around the house will help everybody feel better and become more balanced.

One of the most dramatic stories of the effect of the flower remedies is that of a horse named Reina. Reina is a beautiful Paso whose person just could not relate to her. They always seemed at odds. Reina would be uncooperative, and her person, Bonnie, was very frustrated. She was ready to sell Reina when something told her to call for an animal-communication session. When I tuned in telepathically to Reina, she sent me mental pictures of her first training experience and how rough on her it had been. She told Bonnie through me that she was angry and resentful of how she was treated and needed help letting go of the painful memories.

Once we learned what the big issues were for Reina, Bonnie created a Bach Flower mixture and gave it to her. Bonnie told Reina that the remedies would help her to release the past and embrace the present. Within two days, Reina was a different horse! Practically overnight, she became gentler, better focused, and more cooperative. Bonnie could not believe the change in her horse. Reina became attentive and eager to learn and to work with Bonnie. Together they trained with ease and created a perfect partnership. Reina happily marched in parades, went on long endurance rides, and performed beautifully. In every way, she became a perfect, balanced horse, handling new challenges with calm and grace.

The Bach Flower Remedies don't work this quickly on everybody. Normally, they take weeks of consistent application to make a permanent change. Typically, human beings need to take them for several months! In our experience, animals respond much more quickly because they don't have as much resistance to being well as we do. The point of this story is that the flower remedies can be a valuable tool for helping create balance in humans and animals alike.

There is no guarantee that the Bach Flower Remedies will completely fix a problem, but we are certain that your animal will feel better mentally and emotionally with the help of the flower remedies.

There are other flower essences available. Some beautiful ones include Anaflora Flower Essence Therapy for Animals, Green Hope Farms, Perelandra Essences, and Spirit Essences, to name a few. (See resources.)

The Bach Flower Remedies—or any flower remedies or essences—are in no way a substitute for veterinary care. They can support you and your animal while awaiting medical help. They can be used in conjunction with all other therapies—holistic and allopathic. As Dr. Bach discovered, the flower remedies support physical healing by balancing and calming the emotions. In almost every case, physical healing will be enhanced by flower- essence support.

BACH FLOWERS	KEYNOTES
AGRIMONY	*Positive*: Interior joy, self-accepting, good adjustment, tolerant *Negative*: Repression of emotions, allergies, or irritants
ASPEN	*Positive*: Connected, fearlessness *Negative*: Vague fears, sense of impending doom
BEECH	*Positive*: Tolerant, acceptance *Negative*: Intolerance, stuck in routine, picky eating habits
CENTAURY	*Positive*: Balanced in relationships, strong in character, positive *Negative*: Meek, victim, harassed by other animals
CERATO	*Positive*: Certain, strong, steady, self-confident *Negative*: Inattentive, distractible
CHERRY PLUM	*Positive*: Calm, quiet, in control, makes good choices *Negative*: Loss of control, destructive, overstressed, territorial, aggressive
CHESTNUT BUD	*Positive*: Speed in learning lessons or breaking habits, attentive *Negative*: Stubborn in chewing or chasing, stuck in patterns
CHICORY	*Positive*: Selfless care, generosity, unconditional love *Negative*: Possessive, clinging, manipulative, congestive
CLEMATIS	*Positive*: Conscious and focused *Negative*: Inattentive, indifferent, listless, lonesome
CRAB APPLE	*Positive*: Cleansing of infections and emotional or physical toxins *Negative*: Persistence of infections or attitudes, shame, abandonment
ELM	*Positive*: Capable, responsible, strong, adaptable *Negative*: Overwhelmed or nervous fatigue

BACH FLOWERS	KEYNOTES
GENTIAN	*Positive*: Restoration of hope, rehabilitation from long illness *Negative*: Setback, disappointment
GORSE	*Positive*: Faithful, hopeful, positive thinking, vibrant *Negative*: Hopelessness (giving up with cancer, or after a critical injury or surgery)
HEATHER	*Positive*: Attentive, selfless, helpful, balanced, satisfied *Negative*: Lonely, needy, clingy (annoying need to be the center of attention)
HOLLY	*Positive*: Generous, able to share, interior harmony, tolerant *Negative*: Angry, aggressive, jealous, neglected, abused, need for love
HONEYSUCKLE	*Positive*: Support during loss, replenishment (acting in the present) *Negative*: Grief, homesickness, depletion of energy, isolation
HORNBEAM	*Positive*: Certain, energetic, quick of mind *Negative*: Mental or physical weariness
IMPATIENS	*Positive*: Patient, soft, free from pain *Negative*: Impatient, irritable, nervous energy, pain
LARCH	*Positive*: Confident, safe, secure *Negative*: Lack of self-confidence, insecure, abused, confusioned
MIMULUS	*Positive*: Fearless, courageous *Negative*: Timid, specific fears (illness that does not respond to treatment)

BACH FLOWERS	KEYNOTES
MUSTARD	*Positive*: Serene, joyful, stable, peaceful *Negative*: Depressed, gloomy (mood swings)
OAK	*Positive*: Strong, dependable, trustful *Negative*: Chronic exhaustion (overworked but still struggling; loss of control)
OLIVE	*Positive*: Good recovery, vital, endurance *Negative*: Physical exhaustion from long strain or old age
PINE	*Positive*: Responsible, humble, confident *Negative*: Perfectionism, guilt (feeling rejected, abused, and never succeeding)
RED CHESTNUT	*Positive*: Positive, calm (trusting life) *Negative*: Worry, anxiety for others
ROCK ROSE	*Positive*: Courageous, strength of character, faithful, trusting *Negative*: Terror, panic
ROCK WATER	*Positive*: Flexible, willing, joyful, aware of big picture *Negative*: Inflexible, picky, stiff (arthritis)
SCLERANTHUS	*Positive*: Balanced, determined *Negative*: Imbalanced, uncertain (neurologic or hormonal problems, motion sickness)
STAR OF BETHLEHEM	*Positive*: Peaceful, calm, comfort from trauma *Negative*: Mental, physical, or emotional shock; deep fear; pain (for any stray or shelter animal)
SWEET CHESTNUT	*Positive*: Faithful, trustful, freedom through understanding Negative: Despair, burnout (at one's wits' end), claustrophobic

BACH FLOWERS	KEYNOTES
VERVAIN	*Positive*: Wise, balanced, relaxed, peaceful, calm *Negative*: Intense, hyperactive, overenthusiastic (constant barking)
VINE	*Positive*: Understanding, loving, patient, shows respect for others *Negative*: Controlling, dominating, bossy
WALNUT	*Positive*: Stable, transitions well, protective (good boundaries) *Negative*: Oversensitivity to humans, environment, or change
WATER VIOLET	*Positive*: Tranquil, peaceful, joyful, wise *Negative*: Grieving, reclusive, arrogant
WHITE CHESTNUT	*Positive*: Focused, clarity, determined *Negative*: Preoccupied , obsessed (repetitive thoughts)
WILD OAT	*Positive*: Clear understanding of roles, feeling useful *Negative*: Bored, destructive, feeling useless, underutilized
WILD ROSE	*Positive*: Joyful, content, accepting ("being here now") *Negative*: Apathetic, passive resignation
WILLOW	*Positive*: Optimistic, responsible, accepting *Negative*: Resentful, destructive (ignoring others out of anger)
RESCUE REMEDY	A five-flower combination for any acute shock, trauma, or stress. Contains Cherry Plum, Clematis, Impatiens, Rock Rose, and Star of Bethlehem. Considered a single remedy when mixed.

THREE

Natural Techniques
for Balanced Living

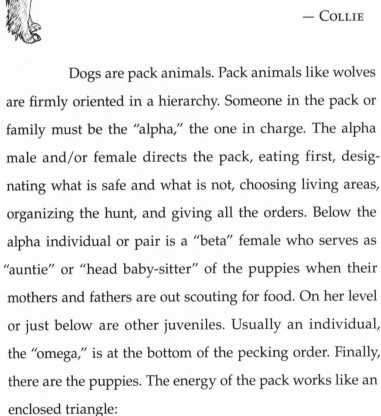

CHAPTER 7

Dogs

Boundaries are structure. Structure is form.

Form is substance. Substance is purpose.

The purpose is Love.

— COLLIE

Dogs are pack animals. Pack animals like wolves are firmly oriented in a hierarchy. Someone in the pack or family must be the "alpha," the one in charge. The alpha male and/or female directs the pack, eating first, designating what is safe and what is not, choosing living areas, organizing the hunt, and giving all the orders. Below the alpha individual or pair is a "beta" female who serves as "auntie" or "head baby-sitter" of the puppies when their mothers and fathers are out scouting for food. On her level or just below are other juveniles. Usually an individual, the "omega," is at the bottom of the pecking order. Finally, there are the puppies. The energy of the pack works like an enclosed triangle:

```
        /\
       /  \
      / Alpha\
     /  pair  \
    / Beta female\
   / and young adults\
  /    Omega    \
 /    Puppies    \
/_____\
```

Within the triangle is a secure structure and an appreciation of every individual's contribution to the whole. The structure provides safety and hunting efficiency, harmony, and balance for every wolf's happiness and survival.

When a canine lives with a human or humans, it is critically important for a human to be the "alpha" in the "pack." The human alpha must always remember to be loving, respectful, and very careful not to humiliate or brutalize the dogs in his care. The human (or human pair) needs to give consistent and clear messages or the dog will not accept them as the alpha. In a canine pack, the alpha male and female are always clear, direct, and consistent. Any other type of behavior is simply not alpha. Their goal is to instill security, confidence, and cooperation among all pack members. If the human is not the alpha, someone must be, so the dog takes over. This can result in aggressive, possessive behavior, including ignoring directions; stealing food, toys, and clothing; and destroying things. A wishy-washy human can create an insecure dog, resulting in shy, frightened behavior or fear-based aggression. How a dog manifests his discomfort with the lack of alpha authority depends on the individual dog, as well as breed and/or past experience.

You must be the benevolent alpha in your pack if you want a happy, peaceful human/canine family. Always be consistent, clear, and direct with your dog, as well as respectful of her as your friend and companion for life. Make rules and stick to them. For everybody's safety and security, do some basic training together: sit, halt, down, stay, come. Avoid trainers and training techniques that instill fear or use dominance and control. In the hands and minds of certain human beings, the alpha wolf concept has been distorted into an excuse for abuse. We do not accept choke collars, prong collars, "alpha rolls," screaming at your dog, hanging a puppy from a leash, and so on, as training techniques. Stop and ask yourself, how would you respond if the person you love treated you this way? Fortunately, there are more enlightened techniques available that will bring joy and partnership rather than dominance and control to your relationship. If you love, respect, and treat your dog honorably, your dog will love and respect you, feel safe and secure, and be a good citizen.

Before you bring a puppy or new dog into your home,

read *The Tao of Bow Wow* by Deborah Wood. This is the gentlest, most respectful book that we have ever encountered on creating loving, secure partnerships with dogs, including positive training techniques. If you can buy only one dog training book, *The Tao of Bow Wow* should be the one! (See the resources for details, and other positive training options.)

Mother knows best. All puppies are instinctively oriented toward their mothers. If you observe a mother dog's communications and emulate them, your puppy will learn quickly. Mother dog strives to get her puppy's attention in order to teach him pack rules, boundaries, and safety. This is not discipline or punishment. If you are effective at lovingly utilizing mother dog's techniques, normally one or two repetitions will be enough to completely stop an offending behavior. Mother dog is patient, up to a point. She moves quickly and decisively if her puppies don't listen. She makes the rules. She's the boss.

It's more appropriate to remove or raise the expensive drapes than try to keep a young puppy from tugging at them. We do not expect human babies to stay out of forbidden cupboards or off of expensive formal furniture. Instead, we use safety latches on the cabinets and create play areas in our homes. Puppies and kittens require the same loving consideration and clear, safe boundaries.

Here's an example of how to respectfully train your puppy by redirecting her. Suppose that your ten-week-old puppy has just chewed up your favorite slipper.

Step one: Pick up the slipper, look at her sternly, and utter a low, "No, no."

Step two: Immediately give her a chew toy, smile, and in a higher, happy voice say, "Good girl, chew this!" Hand her the toy, encouraging her to grab it and chew it.

Step three: Take a moment to play with her with the toy so that she receives both a physical and verbal example of the correct behavior. Under most circumstances, this simple format will allow you to clearly communicate what behavior you wish your puppy to have and what rules you expect her to follow.

Usually a puppy or dog new to your home hears, "No, no, no! Don't chew the slipper! Don't pee on the carpet!" All the dog receives is "slipper," "carpet," and a lot of emotion. It makes a huge difference when you tell your dog what you want instead of what you don't want. Communicate in positive terms whenever possible. Redirect your dog to the activity you want her to do, and reward her for doing it.

Your dog will learn quickly when given positive objectives to follow.

Remember that your dog is a dog, not a human being. As a dog, she relates to the world differently than you do. Try to see how she sees various situations. Ask yourself how to give a clear, positive message your dog will understand. If you do so, you will understand your dog better and be more successful in training and behavior modification. (See Part Four for more information on interspecies communication.)

THE AFTER-THE-FACT DEBATE

Some trainers will tell you that if you do not "catch the dog in the act," you have to forget disciplining him. Others teach you to "rub his nose in it." Neither of these approaches makes sense from a canine perspective.

Let's start with what you do if you come home and find the chewed slipper. Dogs understand cause and effect. Mother demonstrates this from the start. It's important to demonstrate that your house rule has been broken. After greeting your dog, show the slipper to him and follow the steps above. If you do this with love and clear intentions, your dog will understand and will be less likely to chew another slipper. If you don't clearly demonstrate the rules but show your displeasure, your dog will not understand. He will pick up that you are unhappy but not fully understand why. The communication is unclear. It is likely that more slippers will be chewed until you clearly demonstrate that it is wrong to do so. If you continue to skip the discipline because you didn't catch him in the act, how will he learn?

Rubbing a dog's nose in feces or urine is cruel and humiliating. Have you ever seen one dog do this to another? If you find the soiled carpet after the fact, take your dog over so she can smell it. Notice that your dog will smell the mess well before her nose is in it. Tell her, "I am not happy about this." Take her outside and show her where you want her to go. If you can take the feces out at the same time, do so and place it where you want her to go. Pet her and tell her to always "do her business" outside and that you trust her to remember to come outside the next time she needs to relieve herself. Praise and reward her for listening.

If your house-trained dog begins to defecate or urinate in the house, something is physically or emotionally wrong. Check with a vet for urinary, bladder, or kidney problems first. If there is no physical problem, there is probably an emotional one. Has there been a change in the house—a new person, dog, cat, or furniture? Are you under a lot of stress or "pissed off" at somebody? We have seen many animals urinating or defecating "inappropriately" for very specific reasons. Sometimes a dog is "marking his territory" because he feels insecure or has moved to a new house where other animals lived before. Sometimes a dog does this because he is mirroring or acting out his person's unexpressed stress. Again, if you try to think like a dog, you may understand why he is behaving in a particular manner that seems inappropriate to you. (See Part Two for Bach Flower Remedies to help balance emotional upsets and see my book, *Conversations with Dog* to learn what dogs can teach us.)

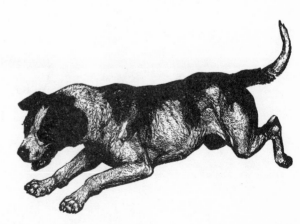

CHAPTER 8

Cats

Healers who are compassionately detached

give the greatest gifts.

— ABYSSINIAN CAT

Cats are solitary by nature. They are not pack animals at all. Their desert-dwelling ancestors lived and hunted alone, coming together only for mating. However, cats are excellent mothers and are affectionate, tender, and very physical with their kittens. The energetic structure for felines is vastly different from the triangle of the wolf pack. In the beginning of a cat's life, the world consists of mother:

Mother

Kittens

After weaning, adolescent cats set out on their own and operate in the world as solitary individuals:

When necessary, or due to selective breeding, some "domestic" cats can adapt to living in family groups—similar to a lion pride—in certain households or for safety, as in feral-cat communities:

This adaptation is not always easy or comfortable for some cats. If your cat is struggling to live in harmony with other cats, first look to his health. A nutritional imbalance can make a cat feel cranky or vulnerable or can cause fighting among cats. If your cats go on the best homemade diet and there are still conflicts after a month of good foods, try the Bach Flower Remedies. If they don't help, perhaps this particular cat simply cannot tolerate living in such close quarters with other cats. Although it may be painful, you should consider finding him a new home where he can be an only cat.

Kittens are very responsive to their mothers and look to them to teach all about life. For example, cats instinctively know how to catch a mouse, but unless mother teaches them how to kill and eat it, they will usually not remember (unless they're really hungry!).

Contrary to popular belief, you *can* "train" your cat. The first step is to establish your role as "mother" or "father." This is most easily done when a cat is a kitten. As you can see in the diagrams, in the beginning of a cat's life, her entire world is her mother. Unlike dogs, who relate to all members of the "pack" throughout different stages of their lives, cats relate to mother first and then become self-focused and solitary once they are weaned. This is why it is easier to train your cat when she is young and still focused on relating to "mother."

Mother cat's disciplinary and training techniques are similar to mother dog's. Like mother dog, mother cat will utilize vocalizations and "flattening." When tiger cubs get too rambunctious, mother tiger takes her big paw and holds down the offending cub until he lies completely still. Then she releases him. She will also pick up her cubs by the scruff of the neck and move them if they are somewhere they are not supposed to be. They quickly get the message.

So how do you translate this behavior to a communication between human and kitten? Here's an example:

Patrice and I were visiting a client with an eight-week-old kitten. The kitten did whatever she pleased, climbing up the arms of the couch, diving into potted plants, and so on. This sort of behavior is cute when a kitten is eight weeks old, but it is unacceptable behavior in an adult cat. It is critical to teach boundaries when a cat is a kitten. A kitten will completely ignore verbal commands, because mother cat teaches with touch. However, pushing or swatting the kitten won't make sense. You have to emulate mother cat's touch.

With the client's permission, I demonstrated the following: When the kitten returned to the plant she had been told to stay away from four times, I went over and picked her up by the scruff of the neck, saying "No" in a low voice. As soon as I grabbed her by the scruff of the neck, the kitten went completely limp. Now she was paying attention! I placed the kitten on the floor, where she lay frozen. While she lay completely still, I told her to play on the floor only and made a picture of this in my head. When I felt that she understood, I petted her from the side of her face, all the way down the length of her little body. This signaled her "release," and she immediately got up and resumed playing, away from the plant. Every human in the room was impressed. I was simply using mother cat's training techniques. Petting the kitten from face to tail is the human version of a mother cat's tongue stroking and expressing her love, acceptance, and approval.

"Scruffing" a kitten is only accepted until they are about eight weeks of age—about the time a mother cat can no longer carry them around. After that age your cat will get very angry if scruffed!

It is very important to do this type of training with your kitten. If you don't "do your job" by teaching your boundaries, your furniture and drapes will suffer the consequences. Then usually you have the cat declawed (which is equivalent to cutting off the top of a human finger down to the first knuckle), send him to the shelter, or worse. The human is to blame, not the cat. You have failed as a "parent," but your cat gets the worst of the deal.

Cats will learn, but they will also do just as they please. You will never succeed at military rule with a cat, so pick your boundaries wisely and be reasonable. If you are attached to too many rules and regulations, you and your cat will be miserable. Cats love to "push our buttons." Learning to relax and "go with the flow" is a gift they demonstrate to us. So, enjoy the free spirit you are now living with! (See *The New Natural Cat: A Complete Guide for Finicky Owners* by Anitra Frazier and Norma Eckroate and my book, *Conversations with Cat* to learn more from the cats themselves.)

Cats are naturally curious. Azul, our cat, believes that every new item brought into the house is for his personal enjoyment or entertainment. This includes grocery bags, furniture, new clothes, bed linens, boxes, plants, and flowers. Azul loves flowers. At first we continually discouraged him from jumping on the table to smell or eat the flowers. When we left the house, we put the vase in the bathroom and shut the door in order to avoid spilled flowers and broken vases. Patrice had a better idea. The next time Kate brought home flowers, Patrice took the bouquet and offered it to Azul to smell. With interest and delight, Azul smelled the flowers. We discouraged him from eating any, as some flowers and plants are toxic. Soon he finished smelling the flowers and walked away. We showed him where the flowers would be and asked him to leave them alone. Never again did he jump on the table to "explore" the flowers.

Because cats love to nibble on green things, it is a good idea to grow "kitty grass," which is usually oat or wheat grass, and be sure your houseplants are safe from the cat and, especially, nontoxic. Your local poison control center can provide lists of toxic plants that are dangerous to pets and children. Kitty grass is available in most pet shops. Organic is best, if you can get it.

You will have to reinforce rules many times if you wish them to be adhered to. With a particularly challenging cat, you may have to be more forceful.

When our "teenage" cat, Azul, decided to walk on the kitchen counters, Kate would lift him off with a, "No, please stay on the floor." He ignored Kate completely. Patrice took a firmer approach. When Azul jumped up on the counter, Patrice called his name to get his attention and moved toward him. Azul jumped off the counter with a meow, and then lay down on his side at Patrice's feet. Patrice acknowledged Azul's good choice and petted him. Azul learned quickly to listen to Patrice and responds much better to all of us if we speak in low, clear tones to him.

A cat will show submissive posture by rolling on his

side. This shows you that he is listening and understands that you are angry with him. When he is on his side listening to you, remember to tell him what you expect. Once you have delivered your message, speak softly and pet him to let him know that you love him. Never discipline when you are angry. Your cat will just learn to be afraid of you if you yell and overreact.

Handling a kitten will ensure a good bond. Trim their claws when they are young to get them used to it, but always tell them before you do. This makes a big difference to Azul. When we show him the clippers and give him notice that we wish to trim his claws, he's much more cooperative.

Cats have very sensitive energy fields, and many things we do are interpreted as invading their space. If your cat runs from you or from others, try being quiet and gentle. Do not go after the cat, but let her come to you when she is ready. If she has been rescued from a bad situation, there are Bach Flower Remedies that will help tremendously. Be patient, kind, and loving, and feed good food, and you will receive a happy, well-adjusted cat in return.

THE INDOOR/OUTDOOR DEBATE

There is an ongoing debate over whether cats should be

allowed to venture outside on their own. Statistically, cats who spend time outside unsupervised have much shorter lives than indoor cats. We have found in working one-on-one with cats that the desire to be outside varies from individual to individual. Some cats would rather be dead than be confined to the house. Others are thrilled to be safely indoors. Many are curious and fascinated by the outdoors, eager to be a part of the adventure but scared at the same time. Some individuals are street savvy and have a healthy respect for the predators who are out and about. Others haven't a clue what they will have to deal with.

We feel that the ideal situation is to provide a screened-in enclosure attached to the house or apartment, with perches and great things to scratch, where cats can spend time enjoying the smells, breezes, birds, and so on. The cat is safe from dangers, and the wildlife is safe from the cat. If you choose to let your cat roam, accept the fact that at any time she may not return. Be responsible and spay or neuter your cat. We have found that the wildlife greatly appreciates knowing that the cat will be out. We do this by mentally sending out a warning such as "Attention, everybody! The cat is coming." We also ask Azul to respect the other life forms and to pay attention to his own safety. We have found that cats who have a strong connection to human beings and who are involved in helping their humans heal are generally less interested in being outside. The outdoors represents their wild natures and brings their physical, predatory nature into focus. Being indoors with a conscious human appeals to the higher self, the more spiritual nature of the cat. The more you acknowledge that your cat is a friend and an equal or even a teacher and healer, the more likely it is that he will want to spend time with you inside. Based on our experience, the point is to make a balanced decision. Examine all the factors. What is best for you, for your cat, for the neighbors, for the wildlife? Are you willing to take responsibility for injured wildlife, injured cats, and property damage? Are you willing to accept your cat's predatory nature and/or early demise? Can you provide a safe place? Our advice is to think carefully and make your decision based on what will be for everybody's highest good.

CHAPTER 9

Horses

When you abandon yourself in complete love and trust to another, you arrive to rest in the embrace of God.

— ARABIAN HORSE

Horses are herd animals. Although a herd resembles a pack, horses are prey animals, not predators like dogs and cats. For prey animals, the function of the herd is to provide protection and security and to be the basis of all relationships. There is a hierarchy in the herd, just as there is in the pack. However, the herd is directed by the lead mare, not by an alpha pair as in a wolf or dog pack. The lead mare is the one who decides where the herd goes, who eats and drinks first, and whose babies eat and drink first. She decides on the pecking order. The stallion is the lookout and the stud. His chief role is to impregnate the mares and to stand up to challenges from other stallions. He will also defend the herd if necessary. The lead mare, however, is the one the herd looks to for all major and some minor decisions.

Energetically, the horse herd can be perceived as little circles within a larger circle:

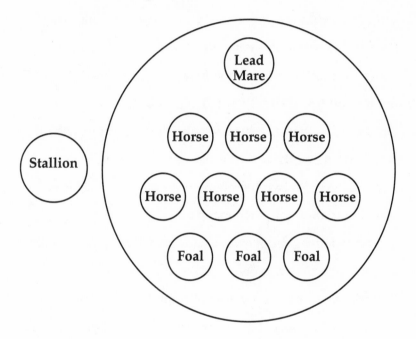

As in a wolf pack, the herd structure provides safety and security. Like individual cats, each horse has its own sensitive energy field to protect it. The lead mare connects everybody together with a circle of energy to protect the whole herd and to detect danger in their environment.

Horses learn respect and trust within their herd structure. Time and intimate experience create bonds and comfortable hierarchies. If a person spends less than six hours a week with her horse, the horse will have a difficult time accepting this person as a herd or family member. If a person approaches her horse like a predator, bossing, controlling, and dominating, trust and bonding will not develop. The horse may accept the dominating control of the human, but love and respect will not be a part of their relationship. On the other hand, a human who spends time with her horse "doing nothing," just being together, will develop a friendship like two members in a horse herd. This is an ideal foundation for partnership and cooperation.

A relationship built on trust and partnership is not just a pleasant alternative to one based on dominance and control. Besides increased cooperation and joy in each other's company, there is a very distinct safety feature inherent in this type of relationship. All members of a horse herd watch out for each other. If a horse accepts her human rider as a member of her herd or family, she will protect her rider. Here's an example:

A client of ours, a small woman, has a seventeen-hands-high event horse. He is a magnificent and beautiful athlete.

He has been trained extremely well to perform a variety of moves in all kinds of situations. Eventing is similar to a human triathlon, except that it is performed at high speed. This woman loves her horse. She talks to him, explains the course, and asks him to participate with her. She respects his intelligence as much as she appreciates his physical abilities. They have developed a bond based on respect and partnership and, as a result, have joyfully won many awards in competition. She has complete confidence in him as a performer and trusts him completely.

One day, they were competing on a difficult course. As they rounded a turn, just before a jump, she began to lose her balance. He felt her body change as fear passed through her. Instantly, he flashed her a mental message, "You get your balance; I've got the course." Without question she focused all of her attention on regaining her balance. Her horse took the jump without missing a step, sailing over it as if nothing was wrong. Because of the closeness between them, a disaster was avoided. She told me that if her horse had not "taken care of her" by holding his course, she would have fallen off and been impaled on a picket fence. In this case, mutual understanding, shared purpose, and a loving bond made the difference between staying on course and serious injury or even death. This is the kind of relationship that is possible when we understand who our horses really are and appreciate that they are capable of making quick, intelligent decisions to protect us, just as they protect the members of their own families.

The training techniques of American Monty Roberts and German Klaus Ferdinand Hempfling have developed from deep respect for the horse, and through their study and understanding of interrelationships within the horse herd, herd protocols, and especially lead-mare body language. The "miraculous" public demonstrations they give of training "impossible" horses are simply an illustration of how to think and act like the lead mare in order to gain the attention and respect of a horse you are training. This knowledge and training technique are not new. Native Americans, Arabian Bedouins, Mongolian tribesmen, and others who depend on the horse for their existence all understand and appreciate how to relate to horses in similar ways. But because "modern" training techniques practiced by most Europeans and Americans for centuries have been based on dominance and control, the methods of Monty Roberts and Klaus Hempfling seem new and revolutionary!

If we truly love and honor our horses, we will learn

how to relate to them "horse to horse" and train ourselves to create a partnership with them, just as Native Americans and Arabian Bedouins did for centuries. Some of the best books on the subject of human/horse partnerships are *Horse, Follow Closely* by GaWaNi Pony Boy, and *The Natural Rider* and *For the Good of the Horse* by Mary Wanless. Read *Conversations with Horse* to understand horses from their perspectives.

CHAPTER 10

Older Animals

Doing a good job is loyalty. Loyalty is love.

— BORDER COLLIE

Young animals learn quickly. Mature animals find their niche in the family and contribute a great deal every day. Elderly animals have unique needs and require special attention and understanding.

Different dog breeds age differently. Many of the typical symptoms of old age—arthritis, incontinence, digestive upsets, kidney problems, poor coats, and failing eyesight and hearing—are not necessarily normal. Many of these symptoms appear because an older animal is no longer able to absorb required nutrients from their processed foods. We have seen dozens of old, weak, and thin animals become vibrant and energetic when their processed pet food is replaced with better foods. Old age does not have to be synonymous with total physical deterioration. Certainly, older bodies have less resiliency than younger ones, but with correct care and feeding they can still remain healthy, active, and bright. As animals age, nutrient requirements change, just as exercise requirements change. An older animal can age gracefully if his human being understands his changing needs and accommodates them. (See Chapter 1 for more information on good foods.)

In a household with more than one dog, a subordinate younger dog may begin to challenge the dominant older dog. This is normal pack protocol. In a wolf pack, the older, alpha male is challenged by younger males to ensure that the leader of the pack is still strong enough to lead the hunt and sire new litters of pups. In your pack, hopefully, the older dog will allow the younger one to "take over," but this does not always happen easily. The older dog may fight for his position and be attacked by the younger one, resulting in possible harm to one or both dogs. If you expect that something like this may happen in your pack, it's important to speak with both dogs. Tell the older one that it's OK to retire, and give him a "new job" worthy of his grandfatherly status. For example, tell your older dog that his new job is to walk with you to the mailbox to get the mail every day. Tell the younger one that his job is to guard the house from uninvited strangers when you are not home. Remember that when you are home, you choose who comes in the door, and your dog needs to obey your signals immediately. (If you've been clear with this when he was a puppy, you'll be fine now.) If you have done a good job establishing yourself as the alpha, your dogs will usually respect your wishes and settle down. If the older dog will not relinquish his dominant status, you must tell the younger one to allow the older one to retain his status in the pack. However, it's OK to let the younger one have some special privileges. If the older dog cannot walk as far anymore, be sure not to penalize the younger one by forcing him to curtail his walks. Make time for each, allowing the younger dog longer, more active walks or playtimes. Be sure to walk your older dog first so he won't feel as bad about being left behind when you take the younger one. Also, because he has had his walk, he will rest more easily when you're out with the other. Tell your older dog you love him, and ask him to watch the house while you're out. Don't make a big deal out of anything. Be clear and decisive, and the dogs will adjust quickly.

These suggestions are not foolproof. Each situation must be handled individually. If the conflict between an older and younger dog is very intense, try working with the Bach

Flower Remedies. Remember to tell the dogs that you are in charge and that you expect them to be respectful of each other. Remind them that you are the alpha and that you accept your older dog in his current state and your younger dog must, too. Usually, once you are clear about what you expect, the tension between them will calm down, and the dogs will establish a new balance.

Sometimes, an older dog (or horse) will feel that her life is over once she reaches a certain point of fragility or vulnerability. This is especially apparent in working dogs whose lives have been very active and directed toward fulfilling particular tasks. It is important to tell your dog or horse that you love her for who she is, not for what she does. Also, tell your dog that as she stays by your side now, she gives you great pleasure. Give her a new job or activity. Tell your horse that you want her to take care of the younger horses and teach them the ropes. Be sure to find a new, less-strenuous activity for the dog or horse to do with you.

Cello is a magnificent German Shepherd who, in his prime, was one of Colorado's finest search-and-rescue dogs. His illustrious career and humble attitude affected the hearts and minds of rescuers and rescued individuals alike. After many years of service, Cello began to slow down. His person, Greta, knew retirement was inevitable. She spoke to Cello about it, promising him that life would still be full—just quieter. As was his style, Cello gracefully accepted the inevitable. However, after experiencing retirement for a couple of months, he became depressed and bored. He lost interest in eating well. He seemed to be giving up and getting older before her eyes. Greta realized that she had to find him a new job quickly. She found out that a local special-education school was looking for a "therapy dog" to be with the children. She felt that Cello might really enjoy being with the kids. She spoke to him about it and decided to give it a try. Cello loved the kids. His quiet, gentle patience won over everybody. With his new focus and renewed purpose, Cello's joy returned. The light returned to his eyes. He began to be himself again. Eventually, he accepted an even quieter life, feeling satisfied to lie by Greta's side as she wrote or played her violin. Just being with the person he loves most in the world is now enough, but it took time, patience, and attitude shifts by Greta and by Cello to arrive together at this place of acceptance, peace, and calm. Every step of the way, Greta supported him and assured him that he was valuable just for being the exceptional being he is. Through her consistent appreciation, positive attitude, and deep love, Cello has been able to relax into his final years and surround himself with satisfaction and contentment.

In our experience with cats, we have encountered what we call the "teacher cat/student cat" relationship. In a multi-cat household, an older, mature cat often teaches younger cats how to "be" with human beings. This older cat sets the example, often eats first, picks his favorite spots first, and holds a strong energy for the other cats to follow and respect. Often, the teacher cat shows the student cats how to cope with visitors or changes in the household, and how to connect with and help heal the human beings in the family. When this teacher cat passes on, another cat will accept his role and continue to set the standard. When you acknowledge this cat's special job, you show him you recognize the gift he brings to your family and let him know you value the role he plays and the example he sets for the other cats.

CHAPTER 11

Tips for Travel

Move slowly with presence and intention and all

creation will show you its beauty.

— TURTLE

It's common for us to worry about our animals when we travel. Of course, the more we worry, the less fun we have. Plus, when we worry, we send "negative" thoughts to our animals that can cause the very problems we hoped would not occur! Here are some tips to help you help your animals when you travel.

1. The best choice for most animals is to be able to stay in their own home with a house-sitter. If you can arrange this, great!

2. The next best solution is usually a pet-sitting service. Pet-sitters will come to the house one to three times a day to walk, feed, and play with your animals. Be sure to introduce the pet or house-sitter to your animals before you leave. Engage the pet-sitter in a favorite game with the dog(s) or cat(s). With a

particularly suspicious animal, allow the pet-sitter to give a favorite food or treat. This goes a long way as an "icebreaker." Remember to tell your house rules to the dogs and cats as well as to the pet-sitter, and let everyone know that you trust them to behave normally.

3. Another alternative is to send your dog or cat to a friend's house. If your companion is familiar with the person and their animals, it's like summer camp and is fun for everybody. A situation like this can be even better than a house-sitter!

4. A kennel can work, especially if your dog likes other dogs. Be sure you visit the facility a couple of times. Go unannounced at least once to be sure they are what they say they are. Observe the state of the dogs in the kennel. Are they happy or stressed? What is the overall feeling of the place? Is the staff happy and pleasant? Is the kennel clean and bright? Are there good, clean exercise or play areas? Get references and follow up. When you take your animal to the kennel, be sure to take some familiar items: a favorite toy, bed or blanket, and food bowl. Take the food your animal is used to eating. A new, strange food can cause stomach upsets, adding to stress. Another helpful idea is to wear a T-shirt or sweatshirt for an hour or more, and then take it with your dog or cat to the kennel. Having your familiar

smell will reassure them that they are still connected to you. Don't take all their toys, because if you do, the dog or cat may feel that you are sending them away for good. Be sure to tell them that they will be in the kennel for whatever number of days and that you will pick them up and bring them back home. Try to kennel your dogs in the same run or next to each other. Try to kennel cats in a facility designed just for cats. Barking dogs will cause a great deal of stress for cats forced to be away from home.

5. Boarding animals at the vet is not usually pleasant for the animals. How would you like to stay at a hospital while your family was on vacation? The staff's priority is tending the sick and injured animals, and they usually have little time for animals who are boarding. Your animals will pick up the fear and trauma of the sick and injured animals. They will know that someone is dying or has died. They may begin to feel that they could get sick or die as well while in this environment. A boarding kennel designed for short stays carries a specific energy since all the animals are there for limited periods of time. The staff is there to care for your companion animals while you are away. Your message of being away for a specific time is reinforced by the other animals' experiences. This supports your animal instead of frightening him.

6. Never try to sneak out. Your dog or cat will know what's up. Being dishonest will sadden them and create further upset. Instead, tell them you are going on a trip. Tell them how many days you will be away. Tell them you love them very much and want them to be happy, stay safe, eat well, and be fine while you are gone. Let them smell the suitcases and check out your clothes and effects. When it's time to leave, say good-bye with a smile and ask them to take care of the house while you're away.

7. While you are away, take a moment just before you fall asleep at night or when you first wake up in the morning to connect with your animals. While you are lying quietly in bed, imagine them well-fed and sleeping peacefully in a favorite spot or playing with a favorite toy. Tell them mentally that you are fine and having a lovely time, just as you wish they are. Tell them that you will see them in (for example) six days. The next day, repeat the process, telling them that you will be home in five days, and so on. If you feel that it makes more sense, tell them you'll be home after six dinners, instead of six days. People who have tried this technique report that it really helps the animals. And it always helps the human feel better. House-sitters familiar with particular animals have reported that when the companion human sent this long-distance message, the animals

acted calmer, ate better, and seemed more relaxed. Try it!

The best way to create clear, successful communication with the animals in your life is to appreciate who they are as animals and to remember that they are intelligent, sensitive beings. Respect their physical selves and appeal to their "higher" or intelligent selves, and you will develop the richest and most rewarding relationships possible.

FOUR

Interspecies Communication for Balanced Relationships

CHAPTER 12

Who Are Our Companion Animals?

All of us are connected by our commitment to honor one another in every moment of every day. This is the key to living life in truth and dignity.

— WOLF (DOG'S ANCESTOR)

In the preceding chapters, we have covered balanced bodies, balanced emotions, and balanced living situations. Now we come to the next step in deepening our partnerships with the animals in our lives—communication. Most people believe that there are only two options open to us for communication with animals—spoken commands and body language. Happily, there is another more sophisticated, more sensitive, more in-depth option available to us. It is telepathic communication. Telepathy is defined in the dictionary as "communication of facts, feelings, impressions between mind and mind at a distance."

Animals are intelligent, feeling beings. They communicate by exchanging thoughts in addition to body language, vocalizations, scenting, marking, and so on. Because animals cannot speak in words, most humans seem to believe that they cannot think. (An animal might argue, because humans speak, they have lost the ability to think!) Because we can speak, most of us have lost the ability to exchange thoughts. The good news is that most of us can regain this ability, at least to some extent.

Telepathy is a direct link to the pure thoughts of another being. When we communicate mind to mind, our sense of superiority and separateness fades away and is replaced by a sense of kinship with all that is around us. All of us in "civilized" societies are trained as children to believe that telepathy is the stuff of science fiction and fairy tales—such as *Star Trek* and *Dr. Dolittle*. However, telepathy is another sense we possess, one that lies dormant from disuse. Through exercise and practice, many of us can reawaken this sense and reestablish our kinship with nonspeaking beings on our planet.

According to our personal experience and the experience of many others who share our profession, animals frequently think in mental pictures. Their worlds consist of images, feelings, sensations, and experiences along with instinct and protocols. One of the first tools you will need to develop is the ability to form and transmit visual pictures. When you practice forming pictures in your mind and sending them to your companion animal, you will find that your animal learns very quickly. Remember to think of the positive thing you wish to see. As we mentioned in Part Three, if you worry about the puppy chewing the new carpet, you can literally plant the idea in her head. Instead, visualize her happily munching on her chew toy.

The major barrier to communicating with animals is our own minds—our conditioning, emotions, distractions, preconceived ideas, belief systems, and denial. Another deterrent is our inability to quiet and focus our minds, unless we have learned to meditate or concentrate. The creation of a quiet mind takes practice. Once we have learned this, we must develop a state of expanded awareness. This means we must move beyond ourselves to realize that we are a part of all that is. Our companion animals are eager to help us learn how to embrace these ideas.

The dog, the cat, and the horse have a very special relationship to humanity. We have learned that these three species have taken on a Service commitment to the Divine. In this "contract," they have agreed to form a sacred partnership with human beings to help us find our way back Home

—back to Source, back to God, back to Love. Each of these three species has an investment in us, if you will. When individual cats, horses, and dogs are physically healthy and emotionally balanced, they really do care that we also are happy, healthy, and whole. To this end, these animal companions are willing to help the people they love, no matter what the personal cost. When an animal is ill or has an injury, they are often drawing our attention to our own imbalances or a potential problem not yet manifested in us.

Dogs, cats, and horses are individuated souls who grow and develop from lifetime to lifetime, just as we humans do. The idea of reincarnation was foreign to me until I started listening to animals. But over the years, their memories of previous lifetimes, shared with the people they love, have touched me deeply and caused me to accept reincarnation as real. Throughout many lifetimes, many horses, cats, and dogs work to fulfill their mission of sharing and teaching humans about unconditional love. Each species manifests this gift in a slightly different way.

THE DOG

The dog is pure unconditional love. The energy of love is sent directly from canine to human in a horizontal beam of energy. It originates in the canine solar-plexus energy center, in the chest of the dog. This beam is deliberately directed to our heart chakra, the energy center of our heart. The solar-plexus center of the dog corresponds to the heart chakra of the human in that each is the energetic seat of love, compassion, trust, loyalty, devotion, forgiveness, acceptance, and peace. When the dog sends a beam of love from his solar-plexus center to our heart chakra, we are bathed in this love, and our own love (of self and others) is strengthened. It is through the exchange of love that both human and canine grow in understanding and partnership. One dog described it thus: "I am the rug beneath your feet that buffers you from all the harshness of life."

THE CAT

The cat is detached love. Cats work with a vertical beam of energy. They are connected to Source and to the Earth in a beam of Light. They model this connection for us every day and teach us that we do not need to stay separated from Source while living in form. They teach us how to live simultaneously balanced on the Earth and connected to God. Cats teach harmony, balance, and high healing. Cats are extraordinary healers. Healthy cats are able to take an illness from a human or another animal, energetically transform it, and release it, without getting sick themselves. Many therapists and massage practitioners have cats who insist on being in their treatment rooms. These cats are working with practitioners to strengthen their ability to heal, as well as helping to transform and release the emotional, spiritual, and physical imbalances of patients. Through the quality of detachment, cats model an excellent way to love and to heal. Humans are notorious for our attachments, expectations, and fears. A balanced cat has little patience for these qualities, but is willing to live with us to show us another way of being.

THE HORSE

The horse has perhaps the toughest job of all. Horses are with us to teach trust. Most people, however, learn to ride or work with horses through dominance and control. When the relationship between a horse and a human is built on dominance and control, trust cannot develop. We have heard that horses are sold an average of once every four years, so they may live many lifetimes devoid of the special one-human relationship that they crave. It is because of their quality of idealism that they continue to reincarnate to be with us. (Idealism is defined as "persistent hopeful-ness.")

The horse is a being in constant motion energetically. Their energy works vertically as well as in spirals, circles, and ellipses. When a human loves a horse and abandons herself in love and trust to that horse, and the horse, in turn, abandons himself in love and trust to the human, an extraordinary experience takes place. Together, both beings experience a trust and partnership that can create a profound feeling of oneness—a direct glimpse of ecstatic union with God. This is the gift that horses bring to us. How many people working with horses ever allow themselves to receive this amazing gift?

These three species are happy to help guide us into the realms of telepathy and kinship with all life. When we ask for their help and guidance, we acknowledge their missions and help each of their souls to evolve, just as each of ours does. Other animals may be interested in helping us, but they are not as invested in our "getting it" as these three species are. All the other creatures on the planet have interrelationships with each other and with Mother Earth as their top priorities. However, when you truly honor and respect animals of any species and appeal to them for help and connection, most seem willing to do their best. (For further reading, see *Kinship with the Animals* and other books listed under "Interspecies Communication" in the resources.)

> We know that dolphins and whales are highly evolved teachers of cosmic and universal wisdom. Their desire to help humans evolve is not to be overlooked. However, they are a subject for another book!

TUNING IN TO LOVE

Animals can teach us how to understand who we truly are, because we cannot hide ourselves from them. We are not afraid to touch them or to tell them our deepest thoughts and feelings. When we can trust and love ourselves as deeply as our animals love us, then we will understand who we truly are.

So, how do we assist the animals who wish to assist us? The first step is to acknowledge our connection with these beings. By acknowledging that we are equal beings, we

begin to shift our consciousness to embrace the real possibilities. Once we eliminate any feelings of superiority and
accept that all beings have intelligence, we are setting ourselves in motion. To prepare to communicate telepathically
takes deliberate commitment and constant awareness of our
own "disbeliefs." Next, for most of us, it takes practice—lots
of practice. Whenever you doubt yourself, look into the eyes
of an animal who loves you.

CHAPTER 13

Principles of Animal Communication

Listen closely with an open heart and nothing

important will be missed."

— SCOTTISH TERRIER

To understand how animals communicate by thought, it is important to learn how non-physical reality functions. Here is a simplified description: Energetically, between earth and sky, there exists a veil. This veil separates human consciousness from Love, Source, Spirit, God, Creator. Animals experience no such separation. They feel the connection all the time, while human beings struggle to find it and to remember their divine nature.

To telepathically communicate with animals, one must enter into their reality of "oneness." For many people, the sensation of oneness and unconditional love can be overwhelming at first. This is why the dog, cat, and horse devote themselves to helping us connect and remember. If a person is willing to connect with unconditional love and oneness, the possibilities for interspecies communication open wide! However, the path to this holy place is littered with our fears, expectations, traumatic experiences, education, belief systems, and so on. Most of us have to learn to release this "baggage" in order to feel secure and at home in unconditional love. To that end, we (and others in the same or similar professions) teach human beings how to release this old "stuff" in order to find their authentic, true selves, free from past experiences, doubts, and fears. Recognizing one's baggage and learning how to deal with it is, for us, the foundation of clear telepathic communication. Without an ongoing commitment to personal awareness, the process of opening to receive telepathic communication can be confusing, scary, and overwhelming. Without personal clarity, the information received can be clouded and distorted.

To create a good foundation in "knowing yourself," we urge you to read and explore spiritual- and personal-growth teachings. Unconditional love and a healthy mind, body, and spirit are everybody's birthright. Find your own true path, and stay on it. If you need guidance, visit your local bookstore's section on spirituality and personal growth. Visit the Web. Attend lectures and take workshops. Become aware of every choice you make. Remember, we have only one real choice: love or fear. When you find your true, love-filled self, you will become a beacon of light for your fellow humans and animals, who will be so pleased that you woke up and remembered who you really are!

Following are the steps we use to teach people how to open their intuition and reawaken their ability to communicate with animals. The steps are given in outline form. By using them, you could succeed in profoundly changing your relationships with all the beings in your life!

HOW TO PREPARE FOR ANIMAL COMMUNICATION

1. Believe that it is possible: Yes, I can!

2. Know your own mind.

   a. Quiet the mind; focus on your breath, and observe your busy mind.

   b. Examine your assumptions and expectations.

3. Eliminate distractions.

   a. Remove physical noise and extraneous activity around you.

   b. Clear out your emotions and personal agendas.

4. Learn discernment—ask if what you receive makes sense, if it is helpful and positive for all.

5. Trust what you receive—this is inner respect, which takes you back to number 1.

6. Keep track—keep a journal, and record every little feeling or thought, no matter what.

7. Practice.

Organized preparation will allow you to set a time to practice every day or every other day. Keeping a journal will show you how much progress you're making and help keep you motivated.

THE FOUR LEVELS OF CLEAR COMMUNICATION

In our experience, there are four levels of clear communication:

1) Clear Thinking

2) Clear Connection

3) Clear Development

4) Clear Speech and/or Action

The first level: Clear Thinking means that we must be aware of and set aside our own opinions, assumptions, expectations, desires, and fears. If we are unaware of any of these or give into any of these, the information we receive will become tainted, and we will inaccurately represent the animal. The steps to Clear Thinking are:

A) Set the intention to be an open and clear conduit for the animal.

B) Be aware of your opinions, assumptions, expectations, desires, and fears.

C) Decide if you can remain clear of these for the duration of the session. If you cannot, respectfully tell the guardian that you are not clear and do the session when you are.

The second level: Clear Connection must be made with the animals *and* their guardian. We accomplish this with the intention of honoring their relationship and detaching from any emotional charges between the animal and human or those around an issue or problem.

A) Set the intention to honor each being in the relationship.

B) Detach from the situation and any emotions present.

C) Respectfully approach the animal. Touch only if invited by the animal.

The third level: Clear Development means that we must form our words carefully in partnership with the animal in order to stay open and focused on what the animal wishes us to express for him. We must be discerning without being judgmental.

A) Offer yourself to the animal to express what he wishes you to.

B) Make no new opinions or judgments.

C) Allow the information to flow through you.

The fourth level: Clear Speech and/or Action means that we must speak and act with the highest intention—for the animals' and humans' highest good. With our loving compassion, we help support the relationship between the animal and the guardian. In this way, we set up the best environment for clarity and healing on all levels.

A) Set the intention to speak and act for the greatest good of all.

B) Remain in a compassionate, detached place.

C) Allow the animal to speak through you. Trust him to help you choose the best words for and delivery to his guardian

D) Finish by asking the animal and human if they have any more to say.

E) Close the circle by thanking the animal and the human for inviting you to help them communicate more clearly with one another.

Following these steps within the four levels of clear communication will provide you with a strong foundation for receiving information and accurately delivering what you receive. The next set of steps provide more check points for regular practice.

STEPS TO SUCCESSFUL COMMUNICATION

1. Respect animals as equal beings, not better than or worse than you.

2. Ask permission—first verbally, then later by assuming an attitude of respect. An animal will recognize and appreciate this immediately.

3. Assume an attitude of peacefulness, gentleness, and openness.

4. Alignment—touch or no touch? Follow the animal's lead. Enter gently into their space, play with them, sit quietly, and so on.

5. Open the receivers in the body—quiet mind, peaceful body. A gut-wrenching feeling can mean that emotions are obstructing clear communication. Check your feelings and expectations. Find a neutral, centered space within yourself and continue.

6. Wait. Focus on passive receiving, not holding on to an expected or desired answer.

7. Ask for an answer—and include a request that the information shared be for everybody's highest and greatest good. This will help ensure that accurate and valuable information is exchanged.

8. Listen. (Receiving nothing may just mean "not now.")

9. Express what you observe, feel, or receive. Speak to someone supportive, write in your journal, and so on.

10. Thank the animal, and then complete and close the circle.

HOW COMMUNICATION ARRIVES

Nonphysical communication often arrives to us in the same manner as physical communication. For example, most of us are very visual. We are used to seeing words, colors, shapes, movement, objects, television, film, and so on. How do you correlate these images with nonphysical communication? You might "see" with the mind's eye a picture of an event, like a puppy playing ball with a boy. Look at the following list and think of examples of how the physical communication manifests. Then transform the sense to the nonphysical.

PHYSICAL	NONPHYSICAL
Visual (seeing)	Clairvoyance
Auditory (hearing)	Clairaudience
Kinesthetic (touch and feeling)	Empathy

In the nonphysical realm, we also receive via:

- Dreams

- Telepathy, or "thought drops," also known as clairsentience

- Combination of the above—most of us receive information in combinations

Again, this outline is only an introduction to creating a new relationship with your animals. For more in-depth study and practice, see the resources for books and workshops.

WHEN ANIMALS COMMUNICATE WITH US

Animals are sending thoughts, pictures, and feelings to us all the time. We are the ones who must learn how to pick them up. Although many of us are best at receiving visual information, we are all receiving much more. Typically information comes to us in combinations or *blends*. For example, visual information gets mixed with feelings or sensations, smells mixed with memories. We are really holistic receivers. It's important to be open to all ways of receiving.

Here's an example of a strongly visual communication mixed with thoughts, feelings, and memories. One time, I was called in to consult with a Standard Poodle with many accomplishments to her name. After brief introductions, her person got right to the point. She asked me why her poodle, who was an expert tracker, never performed well in the obedience ring. The woman further explained that she found this strange because tracking was much more complicated and required much more thinking on the dog's part than obedience work.

I looked at the dog, and she sent me a picture of her and her guardian working fabulously as a team tracking in the field. Dog and human were focused together on the same goal and the dog felt competent and supported by her person. Next, she sent me a picture of her and her guardian in the obedience ring. The woman was anxious, sending thoughts to the dog that she didn't believe the poodle would do the task "right." The dog, so tuned into her person, clearly received the thoughts and images from the human being, even though the person didn't realize she was "sending" anything. The dog then sent me the following words, "I get so confused. She tells me she wants me to do well at obedience, but in her mind, she sees me failing." As the dog sent me these thoughts of her own, I simultaneously received the uncomfortable mixed message the dog received from her person in the ring. The person actually saw the dog failing in her mind before the dog even started the exercise. The dog felt uneasy with this duality and made the decision to respond to the visual messages she was receiving from her person instead of the verbal ones.

I turned to the guardian and said, "When you two are

tracking together, you are working in a seamless partner-ship. You and your dog share the same focus and intent. Your dog feels your support and is completely clear on what she needs to do and how to do it. On the other hand, in the obedience ring, you tell her you wish her to do well, but in your mind you see her failing." The guardian thought about this for a minute and replied that that was true. She was so confident with her dog doing the tracking, but for whatever reason, she was afraid that her dog would fail in obedience. I told her to be sure to make a picture in her mind of her dog *succeeding* at each obedience task each time they entered the ring. She promised to do her best since it made so much sense to her. The human realized that her fears were the cause of the problem, not her dog's "inabilities."

The results were instantaneous. The next time poodle and person entered the obedience ring, the person made a picture in her mind of her dog succeeding at each task. She told her what to do and made the picture in her mind match the words that she spoke. Hearing the words that matched the picture, her dog did each task *exactly* as the human visu-alized and explained it. Her person was delighted and the dog was relieved to be enjoying a clear communication at last! Interestingly, the woman told me that if she didn't pay attention and a fear of failing a particular task crept into her mind, her dog would exactly fulfill that picture.

Sending clear, *positive* pictures to an animal is just as important as receiving clear images back. When you practice sending clear pictures of your animal succeeding at any task, you will realize just how much they receive as well as help you learn how to focus. Learning how to focus and send clear pictures and positive thoughts to an animal will show you how well they respond to clear messages and help support you in receiving information back from them. Also, it is always helpful to ask your animal for a physical sign to give you a confirmation.

Once, we were working with a very sick cat. He had been attacked by a dog, infection had set in, and he was fighting for his life. He lay completely still on a futon on the floor. His breathing was shallow and labored. When Patrice gently placed his hands on the cat, the cat began to purr. Patrice sent loving, healing energy through his hands. The cat's breathing relaxed and deepened, and the cat's person immediately noticed the difference. Kinesthetically scanning the cat's body, we picked up that he was using every ounce of his energy to fight the infection and stay alive. As the cat began to breathe deeper, the fight became a little easier. As Patrice continued, we told the person to look for signs from the cat that he was winning the fight. We told her that when a sick cat begins to groom himself again, he's showing that he's feeling better. Minutes after we said this, the cat lifted his head and licked his paw. Everybody was impressed.

Patrice continued to lay his hands on the cat. We picked up from the cat that he used his tail very expressively and asked his person if this was so. She answered that his tail told her exactly how he felt about things. Different movements conveyed different feelings. The entire time we had been with the cat, his tail hadn't moved. Patrice suggested that another hopeful sign might be that the cat would move his tail in a way that she could understand what he wished to communicate. As soon as he said this, the cat moved his tail. All of the humans who witnessed this remain convinced that the cat heard and responded directly to the two of us in order to show us all that he was still alive, listening, and fighting to recover.

Again, ask your animal companion to give you a physical sign that she has understood your communication or that you have understood hers. This will give you important confirmation that you are being heard and understood, and that you are receiving messages better than you think you are.

Thought-based communication, or telepathy, comes through to me as words "dropping" into my mind. This happens when a person is asking specific questions to his animal. I act as "interpreter," providing a voice for the animal to answer with. The human asks the question verbally, I listen, and then I listen to the animal's non-verbal response and speak it rapidly without judging it or trying to "figure out" if it makes sense to me or not. I do my best to keep me out of the way and allow the animal to come through as clearly as possible. As a result, I have difficulty remembering exact conversations because I'm not thinking the answers myself. Again, I'm a voice for the animal, a conduit for the information. Taping sessions provides the best record of an animal's thoughts and words.

Even in this form of communication, I still receive feelings and sensations. Remember, animals perceive through all of their senses—physical and non-physical. It is impossible for them to respond just from their heads as humans do. (Or do we?) Animals send and receive visually, auditorily, emotionally, physically (kinesthetically), and with their minds simultaneously. In order to express all this to the human I'm answering to, I give the words and describe visuals and feelings to the best of my ability. Practice has taught me how to receive on all these levels and clearly express all an animal wishes me to say to his person. My dedication to practice and personal growth insures that I maintain my integrity and commitment to be the best voice for the animals that I can be.

In conclusion, being a clear animal communicator takes time, practice, and commitment to your own personal growth and healing. This is a lifetime journey, not something you can learn and integrate in a weekend workshop. Patrice and I offer an Apprenticeship Program to support people who believe in the value of practice and in addressing their blocks, old patterns, and fears. Please see our Web site, and contact us if you are interested.

TOUCH AS COMMUNICATION

Touch is one of the greatest gifts animals give to us. We love to touch our animals, and they love to be touched. Through touch, we communicate love, affection, joy, gentleness, and compassion. To touch and be touched is our foundation as mammals. If a baby human or animal receives no touch, they wither and die. Touch is critical for health and happiness. Conscious touch is a powerful way to open telepathic communication. When we begin to pay attention to how we touch, and to how powerful our touch is when we are aware that love passes from our hearts through our hands, amazing things happen.

Try putting all your awareness into your hands. Approach your animal lovingly, ask permission, and touch him consciously. How does he respond? Does he look at you differently? Does he relax and ask for more? Or is he surprised that you are focusing so intensely on the touch? Observe what is different between you and your animal when you are consciously touching him.

Cats are very sensitive to how we touch them. Sometimes a cat who seemed perfectly content to be petted on your lap suddenly bites you or jumps off your lap. Why? If you were mindlessly stroking her, she might have experienced an energy buildup that became unbearable at a certain point. Possibly she just got disgusted because you weren't really paying attention. Try being more conscious next time. Odds are good that when you are paying attention, you will feel that the cat is uncomfortable before she has to bite you or leave your lap. She will appreciate your increased sensitivity and awareness, and possibly stay with you longer next time, or as long as you pay attention.

One of the most effective ways to communicate with your animals and actually augment healing is through a special touch technique called the Tellington Touch (TTouch), which was created by Linda Tellington-Jones. Linda, an equestrian, horse-trainer, and animal lover, developed the TTouch after experiencing Feldenkrais bodywork on herself. She figured that if the Feldenkrais method could help her feel so much better, it could help animals, too. Linda began by working on horses. Her TTouch was so effective that people began clamoring to learn it. Horses with chronic fears, illnesses, injuries, and "behavior problems" were experiencing dramatic changes. The TTouch became a powerful healing tool for holistic practitioners, trainers, and owners. Eventually, Linda modified her techniques for dogs, cats, birds, reptiles, and captive wild animals.

Kate first read about Linda's amazing touch many years ago in a story about a python named Joyce. Joyce, an eleven-foot python living at the San Diego Zoo, was experiencing respiratory and other recurring problems, and Linda was called in to see if she could help. Linda had worked on snakes before, but she was eager to learn more. Linda began working on Joyce when she was coiled, but after receiving

Linda's TTouch, Joyce slid off her perch and began undulating into an "S" shape. Finally, she stretched out to her full length. The zoo staff was amazed. Linda tuned in and asked what Joyce needed. Her intuition led her to stand on one side of the python and gently place her hands palms up, side by side, under the python's large body. Linda began doing gentle lifts and moving down the length of Joyce's body. She asked the others to help. Soon everybody was doing little "python belly lifts" along Joyce's body. The python sighed and relaxed. Her breathing changed. Joyce raised her head, looked at everybody, and went slithering off happily. Later, Linda did some more TTouch on Joyce. As she paused on her knees to explain what she had done, Joyce began to slide up Linda's body, finally resting her head softly against Linda's.

Two days later, when Linda was on stage demonstrating the TTouch to more than one hundred people, Joyce was brought out. As soon as she was released, Joyce rushed to where Linda was kneeling. She rose up like a cobra, hovered a moment eye to eye with Linda, flicked her tongue to Linda's forehead, and then slid back down to lie peacefully across Linda's lap. TTouch had created a clear and profound communication between human and snake.

Linda has written *The Tellington Touch: A Breakthrough Technique to Train and Care for Your Favorite Animal* and other great books. She has also created flash cards and videotapes demonstrating how to do the TTouch on horses, dogs, and cats. (See the resources for details.) The TTouch is a powerful tool for creating interspecies communication.

CHAPTER 14

Transitions, or the Death Experience

In dying, we reconnect to Universal Love.

Separation is not real; it just feels that way. Honor

your feelings of grief, but remember that we are

together always with those we have loved.

-- ITALIAN GREYHOUND

Supporting individual animals and their people through the dying process and death is a major part of our work. Animals have great gifts and lessons for us regarding our fear and misunderstanding of death. Time and time again, animals tell their people through us that death is a doorway to another reality. It is not the end but rather a transition back to oneness with Source, before returning to a new body to experience new opportunities. When a human deeply loves an animal, losing him can be harder than losing human family members. This is because the unconditional love our animals bring us is pure and very clear, unlike what most of us experience in our complicated human relationships. How do we transform guilt, grief, pain, and loss? It is not easy, but if we listen to our animals, we can begin to understand and integrate the process. Here's what to do when you believe that your elderly or ill animal may be preparing to die:

- Follow your intuition and trust that you will choose what is best for your animal. (Sometimes you will disagree with the vet.)

- Do not be afraid. Animals describe death as a transition, not a final ending.

- Ask for help from your own angels, guides, St. Francis, or whomever you wish to help you and your animal at this time. Ask for guidance for everyone's highest and greatest good. Trust that your request will be answered.

- Release your animal with love. Let go and trust. Remember, you cannot stop the process—you can only prolong it. By "release," we mean give your animal permission to go. If it helps, visualize them going down a tunnel and returning to the Light, to the arms of God, to some person or animal who loved them (or you) and who has gone before, or any image that works for you.

- Do not fear euthanasia. Many times it is a viable option. Ask your animal for a clear *physical* sign that he or she is ready to go. A clear sign would be withdrawing from normal activities, refusing to eat or to get up, the light gone from the eyes. Tell your animal that these signs are telling you that he is complete and ready to go. Tell him when the vet appointment will take place, and give him time to ready himself. If your animal rallies, perks up and eats, that's usually a sign that he's NOT ready. Ask him to complete his life with his family and to let you know when he's ready. Normally, you will see this change take place, and you will be sure when he's ready. Other times, it can be more difficult.

- It is ideal to have a vet come to your home to administer the sedative and final injection. If that is not possible, be with your animal in the exam room and hold or at least touch him when she administers the injection. During the procedure, focus again on Light and Love. This facilitates your animal's peaceful and quick departure. Be sure to tell the other animals at home that you are taking Spot to the vet and that he will not be coming home.

- Plan a ceremony or a private moment with your animal before or after her passing. Tell her how much you love her and what she means to you. If possible, include other animals in the family in the ceremony, if they wish to participate. Again, send the departed animal to the Light with all the love you can muster.

- Find support from others who understand what you are going through. Do not grieve to those who will belittle your feelings. Be kind and loving to yourself.

If you need to have a dialogue with your animal during or after the process, please call us, another animal communicator you trust, or a certified grief therapist whose specialty is companion-animal loss (see "Animal-Communication Workshops and Private Sessions" in the resources). This can be a tremendous help and support.

Good books are available on death and dying. Two authors we recommend are Elisabeth Kübler-Ross and Stephen Levine. Also, Penelope Smith has a lovely audiotape titled *Animal Death—A Spiritual Journey*. Remember that animals reincarnate. Our dog, Mollie, is the reincarnation of a wonderful dog Kate brought home to her family before she went away to college. We have worked with clients to help them reunite with their animal in a new body. The experience of an animal returning to you in a new body will change your view of death for certain!

Lastly, if you are able to embrace the dying process as a transformational experience, you will grow and learn a great deal. As an illustration, we would like to share with you a letter from a client who fully embraced her dog's dying process. We hope it will inspire and uplift you.

Dear Kate,

Abby died early Saturday morning. She began having a very difficult time Friday evening, whimpering and crying. I slept on the floor next to her that night. When she became distressed, I stroked her body and she calmed down. While lying next to her, I told her that this was it — if she still wanted to go on her own, she would have to do it that night. I couldn't let her suffer any longer. After several hours of agitation and restlessness, she relaxed completely, sank her body into mine, and fell into a deep sleep. I held her in my arms, and after she had been sleeping soundly for a couple of hours, I got into my bed next to her. When I woke up a short time later, I found that she had died very peacefully in her sleep — just the way we both wanted it to happen.

I don't know how to express my gratitude to you, Kate, for your help during the past few months. You not only helped me understand Abby's purpose in my life more fully, you also helped me develop a new perspective on the dying process. Instead of experiencing Abby's death with fear and anxiety,

I learned to honor and appreciate the beauty and dignity that accompanies that process. I am very grateful that I had the opportunity to share that process with Abby and yet honor her presence each day while she was still with me.

A few months ago, when contemplating what it would be like when Abby was gone, all I could anticipate was the emptiness that I was sure would fill my heart. I am delighted to report that I do not feel the cold, dark emptiness that I expected. Instead I feel like things have just been rearranged in a way that opens up a whole new brightly lit space within me that makes room for new and exciting things to come into my life — and Abby still occupies a part of that space. With your help, I was able to make the leap to the place that Abby was trying to lead me. I know that Abby was also very grateful for your help in getting me there. I have just completed an incredible spiritual journey.

With sincere gratitude,
Barb

Epilogue

Remember, whoever you are, wherever you roam, always

strive to be the finest you can be.

— WOLF

Thank you for reading *The Holistic Animal Handbook*. For us, it has been a labor of love—love for the animals, and love for those human beings who love animals as we do. We urge you to make a commitment—to your animals and to yourself—to take action with the information in this book. There are many tools here, but they are useless if they remain mere words on a page.

Animals live fully in the moment. They teach us to be present in every moment of every day. Now that you have this information, you have the opportunity to help make every moment of their lives be the best it can be. You now have the knowledge and the resources to develop your understanding and deepen your communication. Go for it!

We welcome comments, suggestions, and questions regarding anything in this handbook. Please feel free to call, write, or e-mail. (See "About the Authors" for contact information.)

Blessings to you and to all the furry, winged, hoofed, scaled, and shelled companions in your life. Enjoy and celebrate the miracle of being together!

Resources

NUTRITION AND HEALTH

The Whole Dog Journal: A Monthly Guide to Natural Dog Care and Training. P.O. Box 420235, Palm Coast, FL 32142; 1-800-829-9165; www.whole-dog-journal.com.

Love of Animals—Natural Care and Healing for Your Pets. (Bi-monthly newsletter). Dr. Bob Goldstein and Susan Goldstein; Earth Animal, 606 Post Road East, Westport, CT 06880; 1 800 211-6365.

Animal Wellness Magazine. 164 Hunter Street, W. Peterborough, ON, CANADA K9H 2L2; 1 866 764-1212; www.animalwellnessmagazine.com.

Save Your Dog! Nourish Him the Way He's Built to Eat. Video. Kate Solisti-Mattelon & Patrice Mattelon, Boulder, CO: SolMat, Inc., 2003; www.AKinshipWithAnimals.com.

Save Your Cat! Nourish Her the Way She's Built to Eat. Video. Kate Solisti-Mattelon & Patrice Mattelon, Boulder, CO: SolMat, Inc., 2003; www.AKinshipWithAnimals.com.

All You Ever Wanted to Know About Herbs for Pets. Mary L. Wulff-Tilford and Gregory L. Tilford. Irvine, CA: Bowtie Press, 1999.

The New Natural Cat: A Complete Guide for Finicky Owners. Anitra Frazier and Norma Eckroate. New York: NAL/Dutton, 1990.

Raising Cats Naturally, How to Care for Your Cat the Way Nature Intended. Michelle T. Bernard. Lincolnton, NC: Blakkatz Publishing, 2003; mbernard@blakkatz.com.

Horse Nutrition and Feeding. Sarah Pilliner. Oxford, England: Blackwell Science, 1992; ISBN 0-632-03239-1.

Natural Nutrition for Dogs and Cats: The Ultimate Diet. Kymythy R. Schultze. Second edition. Descanso, CA: Affenbar, 1998.

Give Your Dog a Bone: The Practical Commonsense Way to Feed Dogs for a Long Healthy Life. Ian Billinghurst et al. Lithgow, N.S.W., Australia: I. Billinghurst, 1993.

Home-Prepared Dog and Cat Diets: The Healthful Alternative. Donald R. Strombeck. Ames: Iowa State University Press, 1999.

Dr. Pitcairn's Complete Guide to Natural Health for Dogs and Cats. Richard H. Pitcairn and Susan H. Pitcairn. Emmaus, PA: Rodale Press, 1995.

The Truth About Pet Foods. R.L. Wysong, DVM. Midland MI; Inquiry Press, 2002.

Reigning Cats and Dogs: Good Nutrition, Happy Healthy Animals. Pat McKay. Revised edition. Pasadena, CA: Oscar Publications, 1998. (Preparing natural diets)

It's for the Animals! "Cook" Book: With the Guided Tour of Natural Care and Resource Directory. Helen McKinnon. 1998. CSA Inc., P.O. Box 5378, Clinton, NJ 08809; www.members.aol.com/IFTA2; e-mail: ItsForTheAnimals@aol.com. (How to prepare and store homemade foods, plus lots of holistic resources.)

Can We Talk . . . Animal Nutrition. Bernie Ryan. (1-916-962-3132) (Raw diet and herbal supplements)

Animal Nutrition: You May Be Poisoning Your Pet Unknowingly, a Little Each Day. John D. Rowe. Bowie, TX: Setter Publications, 1997. (Research into processed pet-food ingredients)

Food Pets Die For: Shocking Facts About Pet Food. Ann Martin. Troutdale, OR: NewSage Press, 1997. (Seven years of research into pet-food ingredients)

Canine Nutrition: Choosing the Best Food for Your Breed. William D. Cusick. Revised edition. Wilsonville, OR: Doral Publishing, 1997.

Four Paws, Five Directions: A Complete Guide to Traditional Chinese Medicine for Dogs and Cats. Cheryl Schwartz. Berkeley, CA: Celestial Arts, 1996.

The Natural Remedy Book for Dogs and Cats. Diane Stein. Freedom, CA: The Crossing Press, 1994.

The Nature of Animal Healing: The Path to Your Pet's Health, Happiness, and Longevity. Martin Goldstein. New York: Knopf, 1999.

Natural Immunity. Pat McKay. 1997. 396 West Washington Blvd, #600, Pasadena, CA 91103; 1-626-296-1122 or 1-800-975-7555; www.patmckay.com; e-mail: home1@gte.net/patmckay/index.html. (Vaccinations)

Complementary and Alternative Veterinary Medicine: Principles and Practice. Allen M. Schoen and Susan G. Wynn. St. Louis, MO: Mosby, 1998.

Homeopathic Treatment of Small Animals. Christopher E. Day. Woodstock, NY: Beekman Publishers, 1999.

Homeopathy for Cats: Healing Your Pet the Natural Way. Richard Allport. Berkeley, CA: Celestial Arts, 2000.

Homeopathy for Dogs: Healing Your Pet the Natural Way. Richard Allport. Berkeley, CA: Celestial Arts, 2000.

Natural Rearing Breeders Directory. Marina Zacharias. Ambrican Enterprises, Ltd., P.O. Box 1436, Jacksonville, OR 97530; 1-541-899-2080; fax: 1-541-899-3414; www.naturalrearing.com; e-mail: ambrican@cdsnet.net. (Directory of dog breeders focused on long-term health and temperament)

Note: As of this writing, these foods are made with wholesome, healthy ingredients. But remember, companies can be sold and ingredients changed, with no notice to the consumer. Stay up to date on processed foods by reading *The Whole Dog Journal*. Good foods are regularly reviewed and changes noted.

FROZEN FOODS

Nature's Variety
www.naturesvariety.com

Bravo
www.bravorawdiet.com

FarMore
www.farmoredogfood.com

Steve's Real Food
www.stevesrealfood.com

Raw Advantage
www.rawadvantagepetfood.com

CANNED AND DRY FOOD

Nature's Variety
www.naturesvariety.com

Innova, California Natural, Karma by
Natural Pet Products
www.naturapet.com

Merrick Pet Foods
www.merrickpetcare.com

Wysong Dog, Cat and Ferret Foods
www.wysong.net

Natural Balance Dog and Cat Foods
www.naturalbalanceinc.com

Newman's Own Organics
www.newmansownorganics.com

Blue Buffalo Bits
1-800-622-0260

Pinnacle Dog Food
1-800-255-4286

ENZYMES

Celestial Cats Feline Enzyme Supplement
Celestial Dogs Canine Enzyme Supplement
(Formulated for raw-food diets)
1-310- 278-1385 or 1-888-CEL-PETS
www.celestialpets.com

FloraZyme EFA, FloraZyme LP, and
FerretZymes Plus, by Pet's Friend
(Digestive enzymes and essential fatty acids)
1-877-239-3552 or 1-305-739-4416

PetGuard Digestive Enzymes
1-800-874-3221

Dr. Goodpet Feline Formula Digestive Enzymes
Dr. Goodpet Canine Formula Digestive Enzymes
1-800-222-9932

ProZyme Digestive Enzymes
(Available through veterinarians)
1-800-522-5537

SUPPLEMENTS

BioSuperfood Bio Algae Concentrate
(For cats, dogs, horses, ferrets, birds, bunnies
and people)
1-303-499-9317
www.AKinshipWithAnimals.com

Calcifood Calcium Supplement for Dogs and Cats
Standard Process Veterinary Formulas
1-800-848-5061
www.standardprocess.com
Also see www.LittleBigCat. com for
ordering information

Celestial Cats VitaMineral Plus
Celestial Dogs VitaMineral Plus
(Formulated for the raw-food diet)
1-310-278-1385
www.celestialpets.com

Celestial Cats Essential Fatty Acid Oil
Celestial Dogs Essential Fatty Acid Oil
(Formulated for raw, homemade diets)
1-310-278-1385
www.celestialpets.com

Call of the Wild
(Poultry-based vitamins, minerals and
enzymes for the raw-food diet)
1-800-748-0188
www.wysong.net

Anitra's Vita-Mineral Mix by Halo Pet Products
1-800-426-4256

Rx Vitamins for Pets
Formuated by Robert Silver, DVM, MS
1-800-RX2-2222
www.naturaldvm.com
(Includes: NutriCalm, NutriFlex, MegaFlex,
Immuno Support, NutriGest, etc.)

Daily Health Nuggets for Dogs
Daily Health Nuggets for Cats
1-800-622-0260,
www.earthanimal.com

The Missing Link
(For cats, dogs, horses, and people)
1-800-774-7387
www.designinghealth.com

FLOWER REMEDIES

Bach Flowers

Kate & Patrice Solisti-Mattelon
Unity Essences
2315A Bluff St.
Boulder, CO 80304
1-303-499-9317 or 1-866-499-9356
www.AKinshipWithAnimals.com

Colorado Canines & Felines Too!
1738 Pearl St.
Boulder, CO 80302
1-303-449-5069
www.coloradocanines.com

The Whole Cat
1540 S. Pearl St.
Denver, CO 80210
1-303-871-0443; fax: 1-303-871-0413

Pet Empawrium
12393 West 64th Ave.
Arvada, CO 80004
1-303-467-7777
www.petempawrium.com

Barbara Meyers, CGT
Certified Bach Flower Therapist
29 Lyman Ave.
Staten Island, NY 10305
1-718-720-5548

Additional Flower Remedies

Anaflora Flower Essence Therapy for Animals
P.O. Box 1056
Mt. Shasta, CA 96067
1-530-926-6424
www.anaflora.com

Perelandra Center for Nature Research
P.O. Box 3603
Warrenton, VA 22186
1-703-937-2153 or 1-800-960-8806
www.perelandra-ltd.com

Spirit Essence
www.spiritessence.com and
www.LittleBigCat.com

E-mail: info@spiritessence.com
(Flower essence therapy for animals)

Green Hope Farms
P.O. Box 125, True Road
Meriden, NH 03770
1-603-469-3662
E-mail: green.hope.farm@valley.net

Master's Flower Essences
14618 Tyler Foote Road
Nevada City, CA 95959
1-800-347-3639
www.mastersessences.com
E-mail: mfe@mastersessences.com

Flower Essence Services
P.O. Box 1769
Nevada City, CA 95959
1-800-548-0075
www.floweressence.com
E-mail: info@floweressence.com
(Retail and wholesale)

INTERSPECIES COMMUNICATION

Kinship with All Life. J. Allen Boone. San Francisco: Harper
San Francisco, 1976.

Adventures in Kinship with All Life. J. Allen Boone and Paul
H. Leonard. Joshua Tree, CA: Tree of Life Publications,
1994.

Kinship with the Animals. Edited by Michael Tobias and Kate Solisti-Mattelon. Hillsboro, OR: Beyond Words Publishing, 1998.

Conversations with Dog, An Uncommon Dogalog of Canine Wisdom. Kate Solisti-Mattelon. Tulsa, OK: Council Oak Books, 2004.

Conversations with Cat, An Uncommon Catalog of Feline Wisdom. Kate Solisti-Mattelon. Tulsa, OK: Council Oak Books, 2004.

Conversations with Horse, An Uncommon Dialog of Equine Wisdom. Kate Solisti-Mattelon. Tulsa, OK: Council Oak Books, 2004.

Communicating with Animals: The Spiritual Connection between People and Animals. Arthur Myers. Chicago, IL: NTC/Contemporary Publishing, 1997.

Animal Talk: Interspecies Telepathic Communication. Penelope Smith. Hillsboro, OR: Beyond Words Publishing, 1999.

When Animals Speak: Advanced Interspecies Communication. Penelope Smith. Hillsboro, OR: Beyond Words Publishing, 1999.

Species Link, The Journal of Interspecies Telepathic Communication. Pegasus Publications, P.O. Box 1060, Point Reyes, CA 94956; www.animaltalk.net.

Talking with Nature: Sharing the Energies and Spirit of Trees, Plants, Birds and Earth. Michael J. Roads. Tiburon, CA: H. J. Kramer, 1987.

Journey into Nature: A Spiritual Adventure. Michael J. Roads. Tiburon, CA: H. J. Kramer, 1990.

Journey into Oneness: A Spiritual Odyssey. Michael J. Roads. Tiburon, CA: H. J. Kramer, 1994.

Behaving As If the God in All Life Mattered. Machaelle Small Wright. Jeffersonton, VA: Perelandra, 1997.

You Can Talk to the Animals: Understanding Your Pet's Complex Emotions. Sonya Fitzpatrick and Patricia B. Smith. New York: Hyperion, 1998.

The Language of Animals, 7 Steps to Communicating with Animals. Carol Gurney, New York, NY: Random House, 2001

The Tellington Touch: A Breakthrough Technique to Train and Care for Your Favorite Animal. Linda Tellington-Jones. New York: Viking Penguin, 1995.

Getting in TTouch with your Dog: An Easy, Gentle Way to Better Health and Behavior. Linda Tellington-Jones with Gudrun Braun., North Pomfret, VT: Trafalgar Square Publishing, 2001.

TTouch for Your Cat. Linda Tellington-Jones. North Pomfret, VT: Trafalgar Square Publishing 2004.

Getting in TTouch with Your Horse: Understand and Influence Your Horse's Personality. Linda Tellington-Jones. North Pomfret, VT: Trafalgar Square, 1995.

TTouch for the Horse, Dog and Cat. Linda Tellington-Jones. (1-800-854-TEAM; videotapes)

The Tao of Bow Wow: Understanding and Training Your Dog the Taoist Way. Deborah Wood. New York: Dell, 1998.

Mother Knows Best: The Natural Way to Train Your Dog. Carol Lea Benjamin. New York: Howell Book House, 1985.

On Talking Terms with Dogs: Calming Signals and Calming Signals Companion Video. Turid Rugaas. Carlsborg, WA: Legacy By Mail. 1-888-876-9364.

The Natural Rider: A Right-Brain Approach to Riding. Mary Wanless. North Pomfret, VT: Trafalgar Square, 1996.

Ride with Your Mind: An Illustrated Masterclass in Right Brain Riding. Mary Wanless. North Pomfret, VT: Trafalgar Square, 1992.

For the Good of the Horse. Mary Wanless. North Pomfret, VT: Trafalgar Square, 1997.

Horse, Follow Closely: Native American Horsemanship. GaWaNi Pony Boy. Mission Viejo, CA: Bowtie Press, 1998.

FURTHER READING

Healthy Animal's Journal, What You Can Do to Have Your Dog or Cat Live a Long and Healthy Life, by Christina Chambreau, DVM
TRO Productions, Sparks, MD; 2003
www.healthyanimalsjournal.com

Best Friends Magazine. Best Friends Animal Sanctuary, Kanab, UT 84741-5001; 1-435-644-2001; www.bestfriends.org.

Medicine Cards: The Discovery of Power through the Ways of Animals. Jamie Sams and David Carson. Santa Fe, NM: Bear, 1988.

Animal-Speak: The Spiritual and Magical Powers of Creatures Great and Small. Ted Andrews. Saint Paul, MN: Llewellyn, 1993.

Animals as Teachers and Healers. Susan Chernak McElroy. New York: Ballantine, 1997.

Love, Miracles and Animal Healing. Allen M. Schoen and Pam Proctor. New York: Simon & Schuster, 1996.

Interspecies Journal. Interspecies Communication, Inc., 301 Hidden Meadow Lane, Friday Harbor, WA 98250; www.interspecies.com.

Communicating with Orcas, The Whales' Perspective. Mary J. Getten. Victoria, BC, Canada: Trafford Publishing, 2002.

Minding Animals, Awareness, Emotions and Heart. Marc Bekoff. New York, NY: Oxford University Press, 2002.

Reason for Hope, A Spiritual Journey. Jane Goodall. New York, NY: Warner Books, 1999.

Ishmael. Daniel Quinn. New York, NY: Bantam, 1995.

Hands of Light: A Guide to Healing through the Human Energy Field. Barbara Ann Brennan. New York, NY: Bantam, 1988.

Emmanuel's Book. Pat Rodegast and Judith Stanton. New York, NY: Bantam, 1987.

Feelings Buried Alive Never Die. Karol K. Truman. Salt Lake City, UT: Publishers Press, 1991.

Reconnective Therapy, A New Healing Paradigm. Herwig Schoen. Santa Fe, NM: RCT Publishing, 2003; www.reconnectivetherapy.com.

You Can Heal Your Life. Louise Hay. Carson, CA: Hay House, 1987.

Shambhala: The Sacred Path of the Warrior. Chogyam Trungpa. Boston, MA: Shambhala, 1988.

The Woman's Book of Dreams: Dreaming as a Spiritual Practice. Connie Cockrell Kaplan. Hillsboro, OR: Beyond Words Publishing, 1999.

ANIMAL COMMUNICATION WORKSHOPS AND PRIVATE SESSIONS

Kate Solisti-Mattelon and Patrice Mattelon
2315A Bluff St.
Boulder, CO 80304
1-303-499-9317 or 1-866-499-9356
www.AKinshipWithAnimals.com
E-mail: solmat@earthlink.net

(Private sessions by phone and in person, workshops, classes, apprenticeships, lectures, books, videos, and flower essences)

Sharon Callahan
Anaflora Flower Essence Therapy for Animals
P.O. Box 1056
Mt. Shasta, CA 96067
1-530-926-6424
www.anaflora.com
(Private sessions, flower essences)

Terri O'Hara
P.O. Box 1027
Kittredge, CO 80457
1-303-670-2020
www.Animalwize.com
E-mail: Animalwize@aol.com
(Private sessions by phone and in person, classes, workshops, flower essences)

Morgine Jurdan
1135 Yale Bridge Rd.
Amboy, WA 98601
1-360-247-7284
E-mail: morgine@tds.net
www.communicationswithlove.com
(Private sessions by phone and in person, lost animals, classes)

Jeri Ryan
P.O. Box 10166
Oakland, CA 94610
1-510-569-6123

E-mail: aiaianimal@aol.com
(Private sessions, lectures, and workshops)

Dawn Hayman
Spring Farm Cares
3364 State Route 12
Clinton, NY 13323
1-315-737-9339
www.springfarmcares.org
(Private sessions, workshops)

Carol Gurney
3715 N. Cornell Rd.
Agoura, CA 91301
1-818-597-1154
E-mail: cgurney@earthlink.net
www.animalcommunicator.net
(Private sessions, lectures, workshops, healing
treatments, training)

Joanna Seere
P.O. Box 93
Warwick, NY 10990
1-845-651-1383
E-mail: joannaseere@spirit-to-spirit.net
www.spirit-to-spirit.net
(Phone sessions, lectures, workshops, healing treat-
ments, training)

Penelope Smith
P.O. Box 1060
Point Reyes, CA 94956
1-415-663-1247

www.animaltalk.net
E-mail: Penelope@animaltalk.net
(Lectures, workshops, training, books, tapes, *Species Link Journal*. No private sessions)

Kristin Thompson
3282 Coormer Rd.
Newfane, NY 14108
1-716-778-6233
www.communcatewithanimals.com
(Private sessions, lectures, workshops)

Barbara Meyers, CGT
29 Lyman Ave.
Staten Island, NY 10305
1-718-720-5548
(Certified Grief and Flower Essence Therapist, hospice, nutrition, behavior, communication arts)

HOLISTIC VETERINARY ASSOCIATIONS

American Holistic Veterinary Medical Association
2214 Old Emmorton Road
Bel Air, MD 21015
1-410-569-0795
www.ahvma.org
(Send a self-addressed, stamped envelope with a request for a listing of holistic vets in your area.)

International Veterinary Acupuncture Society
P.O. Box 2074
Nederland, CO 80466
1-303-682-1167 or 1-303-682-1168

National Center for Homeopathy
801 N. Fairfax, Suite 306
Alexandria, VA 22314
1-703-548-7790

American Veterinary Chiropractic Association
623 Main St.
Hillsdale, IL 61257
1-302-658-2920

International Association for Veterinary
Homeopathy
c/o Andreas Schmidt, General Secretary
Sonnhaldenstr. 24
CH-8370 Sirnach
Leichtenstein
E-mail: aschmidt@access.ch

British Holistic Veterinary Medicine Association
27 Tinshill Road
Leeds
LS167DR
England

British Association of Homoeopathic
Veterinary Surgeons
Chinham House
Stanford in the Vale
Faringdon
Oxon
SN7 8NQ
England

HOLISTIC VETS AND PRACTITIONERS

(Most of these practitioners will work by phone if
you cannot visit them.)

Rob Silver, DVM, MS
Lisa R. Molloy, DVM
Boulder's Natural Animal
685 S. Broadway, Suite A
Boulder, CO 80303
1-303-494-7877
(Chinese herbs, nutrition, Western herbs, acupunc-
ture, Homeopathy, lectures, and classes)

Jean Hofve, DVM
Jackson Galaxy, Behavior Consultant
Little Big Cat Behavior Solutions
P.O. Box 18976
Boulder, CO 80308-1976
1-720-938-6794
www.LittleBigCat.com
(Holistic behavior consulting, Homeopathy,
SpiritEssence flower essences, nutrition)

Amy Norton, DVM
Circle of Animals Veterinary Hospital
15 Colorado Blvd.
Idaho Springs, CO 80452
1-303-567-4757
(Homeopathy and Bach Flowers)

Bev Cappel, DVM
Vet at the Barn
790 Chestnut Ridge Road

Chestnut Ridge, NY 10977
1-845-356-3838
www.vetatthebarn.com
(Immuno-augmentative therapy, Chinese herbs, acupuncture, Homeopathy, chiropractic, nutrition)

Don Hamilton, DVM
P.O. Box 67
Ocate, NM 87734
1-505-666-2091
(Homeopathy and nutrition. Phone consultations only)

Joanne Stefanatos, DVM
1325 Vegas Valley Drive
Las Vegas, NV 89109
1-702-735-7184
(Acupuncture,Homeopathy, nutrition, Bach Flowers, and more)

Christina Chambreau, DVM
908 Cold Bottom Rd.
Sparks, MD 21152
1-410-771-4968
HealthyAnimals@aol.com
(Leading Homeopathic vet, nutrition, workshops, *My Healthy Animal's Journal*)

Pamela Wood, DVM
VCA Wellington Animal Hospital
14471 Southern Blvd.
Loxahatchee, FL 33470
1-561-793-4900
(Acupuncture, Chinese herbs, Homeopathy, nutrition)

Pat Bradley, DVM
65 Sunny Gap Road
Conway, AR 72032
1-501-329-7727
(Homeopathy and nutrition)

Devta Khalsa
Natural Healing for Animals
P.O. Box 314
Ester, AK 99725
1-907-479-9722
E-mail: eaglefeather@mosquitonet.com
(TTouch, Reiki, Pranamonics, nutrition, Homeopathy; brochure available)

SHOPS AND MAIL-ORDER SOURCES

(For good foods, supplements, books, and information)

Whiskers—Holistic Products for Pets
235 E. 9th St.
New York, NY 10003
1-800-944-7537
www.choicemall.com/whiskers

Colorado Canines and Felines Too!
1738 Pearl Street
Boulder, CO 80302
1-303-449-5069
www.coloradocanines.com

Pet Empawrium
12393 West 64th Avenue
Arvada, CO 80004

1-303-467-7777

www.petempawrium.com

Blue Hills Dog and Cat Shoppe
2255 Main Street #117
Longmont, CO 80501
1-303-651-2955

Whole Pets
2900 Valmont Road
Boulder, CO 80302
1-303-444-4733
www.whole-pets.com

Cosmo's, The Retail Store
10210 West 26th Avenue
Lakewood, CO 80215
1-303-232-1477
www.cosmosdogbakery.com

Doggie Dips & Chips
265C East 29th Street
Loveland, CO 80538
1-970-461-1109

The Whole Cat
1540 S. Pearl St.
Denver, CO 80210
1-303-871-0443; fax: 1-303-871-0413

Carousel Outfitters
917 Valley Road
Gillette, NJ 07933
1-908-626-1550

The Critters and Me
1403 Agua Fria
Santa Fe, NM 87501
1-505-982-5040

Avian Medicine Chest
Rt. 2, Box 175
Woodbine, IA 51579
1-712-647-2079
(Homeopathic remedies and more for birds)

Earth Animal
606 Post Road East
Westport, CT 06880
1-800-622-0260
www.earthanimal.com
(Daily Health Nuggets and much more)

Pet's Friend
7154 University Drive #86
Tamarac, FL 33321
1-877-239-3552 or 1-561-391-5615
(Enzymes and supplements)

A Drop in the Bucket
586 Round Hill Road
Greenwich, CT 06831
1-888-783-0313 or 1-888-663-4783
www.dropinbucket.com
(All-natural herbs, supplements, and remedies
for horses)

INTERNET RESOURCES

www.AKinshipwithAnimals.com (Kate Solisti-
Mattelon & Patrice Mattelon)

www.altvetmed.com (Directory of holistic
veterinarians nationwide)

www.LittleBigCat.com (Dr. Jean Hofve's Web site
— Holistic Care)

www.naturalhorsetalk.com (Holistic horse care
resource)

www.blakkatz.com (Holistically raised cats,
vaccination, and raw-diet info)

www.apdt.com (The Association of Pet Dog Trainers)

www.dogmassage.com (Lang Institute for Canine
Health, an accredited massage school/correspon-
dence course)

www.ISPHorse.com (International School for Professional Horsemanship, holistic riding and horse care
school in Belgium)

www.lindatellingtonjones.com (Linda Tellington-Jones,
TTouch classes, books, videos, equipment, etc.)

www.mindspring.com/~woofsportsusa/aafco.htm
(AAFCO ingredient definitions)

www.bestfriends.org (Best Friends Animal Sanctuary)

www.peaceablepaws.com (Pat Miller—positive dog
training workshops, book)

www.flyingdogpress.com (Susan Clothier—holistic dog training)

www.dogwhisper.com (Dr. C. W. Meisterfeld—mutual respect behavior management)

www.api4animals.org (Animal Protection Institute)

www.belfield.com ("Your Animal's Health," an online magazine)

www.dogwise.com (Fabulous source of books on and for dogs—care, training, breeds, nutrition, etc.)

Notes

1. Bob Goldstein, *Love of Animals* newsletter, vol. 5, no. 8 (August 1999).

2. Diane Stein, *The Natural Remedy Book for Dogs and Cats* (Freedom, CA: The Crossing Press, 1994).

3. Association of American Feed Control Officials Inc., *Official Publication* (Atlanta: Georgia Department of Agriculture, 1998).

4. Christine K. Markus, Lawrence H. Chow, Dorothy M. Wycoff, and Bruce McManus, "Pet Food-Derived Penicillin Residue as a Potential Cause of Hypersensitivity Myocarditis and Sudden Death," *American Journal of Cardiology* Vol. 63 (1998): 1154–56.

5. Donald R. Strombeck, *Home-Prepared Dog and Cat Diets: The Healthful Alternative* (Ames: Iowa State University Press, 1999).

6. Jean C. Hofve, "A Pet Food Primer for Veterinarians," working paper, 1999. (c/o Animal Protection Institute, P.O. Box 22505, Sacramento, CA 95822-0505).

7. William D. Cusick, *Canine Nutrition: Choosing the Best Food for Your Breed*, revised edition (Wilsonville, OR: Doral Publishing, 1997).

8. Hofve, "A Pet Food Primer."

9. Lon D. Lewis, Mark L. Morris Jr., and Michael S. Hand, *Small Animal Clinical Nutrition III* (Topeka, KS: Mark Morris Associates, 1990).

10. Helen McKinnon, *It's for the Animals! "Cook" Book: With the Guided Tour of Natural Care and Resource Directory*, 1998. (CSA Inc., P.O. Box 5378, Clinton, NJ 08809; www.members.aol.com/IFTA2; E-mail: ItsForTheAnimals@aol.com)

11. N. Dworkin, "Good Eats," *Natural Pet Magazine*, December 1996.

12. Francis M. Pottenger Jr., *Pottenger's Cats: A Study in Nutrition*, second edition (San Diego, CA: Price-Pottenger Nutrition Foundation, 1995).

13. Joann Stefanatos, "How to Use the Bach Flower Remedies," *Journal of the American Holistic Veterinary Medical Association* Vol. 10, No. 3 (1991).

About the Authors

Kate Solisti-Mattelon, internationally known speaker and teacher, has been a professional animal communicator, communicating telepathically with animals, since 1992. During this time, she has worked with individual animal guardians, holistic veterinarians, trainers, and other professionals, assisting in solving behavioral problems, understanding health problems, healing past traumas, and facilitating understanding between humans and non-humans. Kate has worked with wild animals, learning about their inter-relationships and their roles in balancing the Earth. She has provided advisory support at Fossil Rim Wildlife Center in Texas. She was the guest speaker at the British Association of Homoeopathic Veterinary Surgeons meeting and the Rocky Mountain Holistic Veterinary Association meeting. Kate has been a presenter at Whole Life Expos throughout the western U.S. She also presented a workshop at the International Society for the Study of Subtle Energies and Energy Medicine Conference. Kate has taught interspecies communication workshops in New Mexico, Colorado, Washington, New York, New Jersey, France, England, and Belgium.

Kate writes for *Animal Wellness* magazine on Breed Specific Nutrition. She has also written articles for *Tiger Tribe, Wolf Clan, Best Friends* and *Species Link* magazines. In 1997, Kate co-edited an anthology, published in German, *Ich spurte die Seele der Tiere*. It was published in English as *Kinship with the Animals* in 1998. Contributors include: Jane Goodall, Michael Fox, Marc Bekoff, Michael Tobias, Linda Tellington-Jones, and Michael Roads. She was featured in *Animals, Our Return to Wholeness*, by Penelope Smith; in *Communicating with Animals, The Spiritual Connection Between People and Animals*, by Arthur Myers; and in *Women of Grace, Women Healers & Healing Practitioners*, by Carol Kronwitter. In the fall of 2000, Kate published, *Conversations with Dog, An Uncommon Dogalogue of Canine Wisdom* . This is the first book to ask dogs what they think and feel about living with human beings. *Conversations with Cat, An Uncommon Catalog of Feline Wisdom*, the next book in the series, was released in October 2001. The third book in the series, *Conversations with Horse, An Uncommon Dialog of Equine Wisdom*, was published in 2003. In addition to German, Kate's books have also been published in Italian, Czech, and Korean.

Patrice Mattelon has a gift for hands-on-healing. Both humans and animals benefit from his gentle touch and distance healing. A native of France, he has been a student of Energetic medicine since 1986. A strong sense of intuition has guided him throughout his life. Patrice has studied various healing modalities, including Radionics, Reiki, Egyptian Healing, and Pranamonics. In 1992, Patrice began to develop his own work based on his interpretation of Tarot, Numerology, and the Kabbalah. He now offers this work in a long-distance or in-person course titled "Sur le Chemin de la Lumiere" to supply tools to individuals ready to break through patterns and live the lives of their dreams. He has lived and worked in America since 1996.

Together, Kate and Patrice bring the unique aspect of working as a married couple into the field of Holistic Health for animals and people. Since the summer of 1996, they have been helping human beings understand and nurture the physical, emotional, mental, and spiritual aspects of the animals in their lives for the greatest mutual benefit and growth. Kate and Patrice teach on-going classes on holistic human growth and holistic animal care. Their book, *The Holistic Animal Handbook, a Guide to Nutrition, Health and Communication*, was first published in May of 2000. It was simultaneously published in German as *Spirituelle Partnerschaft mit Haustieren*. Kate and Patrice also offer a long-distance apprenticeship encompassing all areas of their practice.

Kate and Patrice are well respected in the field of dog and cat nutrition. They teach classes on nutrition for dogs and cats at locations in the Denver/Boulder area as well as at the Colorado State University Veterinary College-sponsored SAVMA meeting in March of 2002. Kate and Patrice have produced two videos on dog and cat nutrition, *Save Your Dog! Nourish Him the Way He's Built to Eat* and *Save Your Cat! Nourish Her the Way She's Built to Eat.*

They are regular guest faculty members at the International School for Professional Horsemanship in Meerle, Belgium, and at the Lang Institute for Canine Health in Loveland, Colorado. Kate and Patrice presented their work with animals at the International Forum on New Science, sponsored by the International Association for New Science, in 1998. They lectured and taught at the Whiskers Holistic Pet Conference in New York City in 1998.

Kate and Patrice have been featured in *Synchronicity, Signs & Symbols,* by Patricia Rose Upczak; *Hot Chocolate for the Mystical Lover, 101 True Stories of Soul Mates Brought Together by Divine Intervention,* by Arielle Ford; in *Pets: Part of the Family* magazine (Jul/Aug 1999); the *Rocky Mt. News*

(May 1997 & Sept. 1998); the *Denver Post* (Nov 2001); *Boulder Magazine* (Winter/Spring 2002) and the *Boulder Daily Camera* (July 2003). Kate has been heard on K105 Radio in Denver, ABC News in Denver, and KKTV in Colorado Springs. Kate and Patrice live in Boulder, Colorado, with their cats Azul, Lily, and Simon. Please visit their Web site at www.AKinshipWithAnimals.com.

Index

Tables are indicated by the letter (t) next to the page number.

About Council Oak Books

Since 1984 Council Oak Books has published books from all over the world, books that cross cultural lines to bring new understanding. Drawing from history, we publish for the future, presenting books that point the way to a richer life and a better world. Council Oak Books takes its name from a great oak tree, sacred to the Creek Indians that still grows in the center of Tulsa, our home city. Our books are meant to inspire the sharing of knowledge in the quiet, contemplative space beneath the great Oak.

In keeping with this mission, we publish books on alternative health for animals, as well as the spiritual bond between humans and animals and other innovative titles on the relationship between humans and nature.

See the following pages for a selection of these titles. Please visit our website for a complete list of our current titles: www.counciloakbooks.com or call 1-800-247-8850 to order.

Conversations with Horse
An Uncommon Dialog of Equine Wisdom
$15.95
Hardcover
ISBN 1-57178-157-9
156 pages, 5½ x 7½,
color photographs
Pets & Animals

Kate Solisti-Mattelon
Photography by Tony Stromberg

Professional animal communicator Kate Solisti-Mattelon has proven herself to be a talented and objective translator of what animals have to say. In *Conversations with Horse,* she introduces us to the horse as a living, thinking being with very definite inclinations. You will discover insightful responses from these wise and mysterious beings by reading what horses have to say about:

Do horses like humans riding them?
That depends on the relationship with the rider.

How do you cope with being sold or moved?
It's all in the way we're prepared for the change.

How are you serving mankind other than in the daily work you do for us?
We do not serve mankind.

By reading horses' innermost thoughts and feelings, you will learn how to reestablish the original contract of love, trust, and mutual respect.

Conversations with Horse is filled with answers on how you can enhance your intimate connection with these beautiful creatures. This book is for anyone who enjoys the company of horses.

Conversations with Dog
An Uncommon Dogalog of Canine Wisdom
$15.95
Hardcover
ISBN 1-57178-156-0
156 pages, 5½ x 7½,
color photographs
Pets & Animal

Kate Solisti-Mattelon

In *Conversations with Dog*, professional animal communicator Kate Solisti-Mattelon poses some of life's most intriguing questions to our canine friends. Dogs kindly spell it out with responses that offer insights into the spiritual, physical, and mental awareness of our canine friends. Read their tremendously touching and insightful answers to questions about matters practical and profound, such as:

Why do I love you more than most humans in my life?
We are uncomplicated.

Why do you chase cats?
If it acts like prey, we have to act as predator.

How do you tolerate cruelty and mistreatment and still respond with unconditional love?
We can't help it.

This is not a dog-care manual. It is a tool for understanding. The dogs in your life can be valuable teachers.

Conversations with Dog is filled with inspiration and canine wisdom that will enhance your intimate connection with these beautiful creatures. It is a must-read for anyone who enjoys life in the company of dogs

Conversations with Cat
An Uncommon Catalog of Feline Wisdom
$15.95
Hardcover
ISBN 1-57178-155-2
156 pages, 5½ x 7½,
color photographs
Pets & Animals

Kate Solisti-Mattelon

In *Conversations with Cat*, professional animal communicator Kate Solisti-Mattelon poses some of life's most challenging questions to our feline friends and the cat's responses offer surprising insights into the spiritual, physical, and mental awareness of our feline companions. Cat people will chuckle at the cats' sometimes wry but tremendously touching answers to questions regarding matters practical and profound, such as:

Why do you deliberately sit on the laps of guests who "hate" cats?
Because it's fun to make them squirm.

What is the most important thing we can learn from cat?
Detached love.

Why do so many of you go off by yourselves to die?
Dying is a dance, and God is our partner.

This is not a cat-care manual. It is a tool for understanding. The cats in your life can be valuable teachers, especially if you can begin to follow their example of detached love in your human and animal relationships.

Conversations with Cat is filled with inspiration and feline wisdom that provides answers on how you can enhance your intimate connection with these beautiful creatures. It is a must-read for anyone who enjoys life in the company of cats.

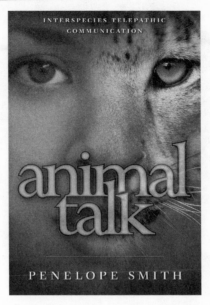

Animal Talk
Interspecies Telepathic Communication
$14.95
Paperback
ISBN 1-57178-149-8
224 pages, 6 x 9
index
Pets & Animals

Penelope Smith

Inside the mind of animals.

Have you ever wondered what your cat or dog or horse is thinking? *Animal Talk* presents tried-and-true telepathic communication techniques developed by the author that can dramatically transform people's relationships with other species on all levels — physical, mental, emotional, and spiritual. It explains how to solve behavior problems, how to figure out where your animal hurts, how to discover animals' likes and dislikes, and why they do the things they do. You can learn the language that will open the door to your animal friends' hearts and minds.

In addition to teaching people how to develop mind-to-mind communication with animals, *Animal Talk* discusses freedom, control, and obedience; understanding behavior from an animal's point of view; how to handle upsets between animals; tips on nutrition for healthier pets; and the special relationship between animals and children.

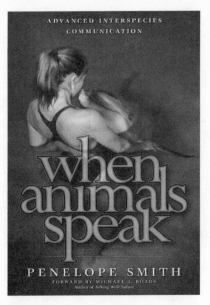

When Animals Speak
Advanced Interspecies Telepathic Communication
$14.95
Paperback
ISBN 1-57178-150-1
224 pages, 6 x 9
Pets & Animals

Penelope Smith

Real-life animal stories to inspire.

When Animals Speak reveals the aspects of animals as our teachers, healers, and guides through deep, life-changing revelations, communicated directly from the animals. Discover who animals and other forms of life really are; how they understand themselves and others; how they feel about humans and life on earth; how they choose their paths in life and death; the depth of their spiritual understanding and purposes; and how they can teach, heal, and guide us back to wholeness as physical, mental, emotional, and spiritual beings. Regain the language natively understood by all species. Laugh as you experience other species' refreshing and sometimes startling points of view on living in this world. *When Animals Speak* is a treasured key to your own intuitive connections with the rest of creation and nature's path to knowing oneself and being free.

Living with Dogs
Tales of Love, Commitment, and Enduring Friendship
  $13.95
  Trade paperback
  ISBN 1-885171-19-6
  224 pages, 5 x 7
  Pets/Human-animal Relationships

Henry and Mary Ellen Korman

A soft muzzle gently brushing against your knee, the companionable wag of a tail, an unabashed bark of delight at your arrival—these are familiar joys for those of us who live with and love dogs. Compassionate, steadfast, and eager to please, our dogs are our friends, companions, and confidants all rolled up into one wet-nosed package.

The relationship between people and their dogs is so powerful that any dog lover, given a sympathetic ear, will share endless stories about his or her four-legged friend. *Living with Dogs* explores the loving connections between scores of dog owners and their canine companions and pays tribute to the everyday joys, adventures, and distinctive characteristics that make these kinships unique.

Living with Dogs is an intelligent, respectful book for the millions of people who count dogs among their best friends, and a loving gift for anyone who answers "yes" to the question: "Are you a dog person?"

In the Presence of Higher Beings
What Dolphins Want You to Know
$13.95
Trade paperback
$14.95/$19.50 Canada
Trade paperback
ISBN: 1-57178-179-X
288 pages, 6 x 9, index
New Age

Bobbie Sandoz

What can we learn from these mesmerizing beings?

For ten years author Bobbie Sandoz swam with a pod of wild dolphins off the shores of her Hawaiian home. *In the Presence of High Beings* is about her remarkable and healing experiences with these dolphins. The first phase of encounters offers a period of friendship during which she learns from the dolphins by observing how consistently they embody the six characteristics of the higher self.

During the second phase Bobbie suspects that the dolphins are attempting to communicate with her. They create "bubble" drawings for her, which Bobbie realizes are the dolphin's way of reassuring her they are truly communicating. When Bobbie opens to receiving their telepathic messages, the dolphins begin to share insights for how humans can release the chaotic world they are currently creating. Dolphins can teach us how to manifest the world of our dreams by showing up for our dreams, playing while we wait for our dreams to arrive, and jumping only for joy — with freedom and grace

In the Presence of High Beings shares the dolphin's formula to rapidly attain a high level of joy. Sandoz also includes a valuable guide on how to swim with dolphins and whales in the wild, and material about healing with dolphin "tapping." Altogether this is a special invitation from the dolphins to join them in their spinning dance to God.